GET PUBLISHED

How to Acquire a Literary Agent
and Land a Book Deal

Laura Cross

Rebel Seed Publishing

Las Vegas | Los Angeles

Rebel Seed Publishing
A division of Rebel Seed Entertainment, LLC

Publishers Cataloging-in-Publication Data
Cross, Laura, 1969 -
    Get Published: How to Acquire a Literary Agent and Land a Book
    Deal / Laura Cross

Cover Design: Lindsay Holt Studio
Author Photograph: Jennifer Wright Photography

TABLE OF CONTENTS

Foreword

I have enough experience to know within one week of working with an author if he or she will succeed in obtaining a book deal. Success is achieved through preparation, hard work, and promotion. To become a published author requires marketing and promotion. Most writers do not market and promote themselves. Why? It takes research, it is sales, it is pitch, it is finding a literary agent—and it takes time and effort to do these tasks.

The craft of writing is a learned process and anyone can learn it. Becoming successfully published is up to you. You are an expert in your field and have a method to share that will change someone's life. You have the craft, now you need to commit to the marketing and promotion.

What exactly is marketing and promotion? In my capacity with helping writers become authors, I can say that it is: to learn the publishing business, mastermind yourself a platform, and romance a literary agent with your perfected book idea in order to acquire representation. It is a long road, but one that is a clear pathway if you have the right sources and resources, and the time to implement them.

Now Laura Cross's book, *Get Published: How to Acquire a Literary Agent and Land a Book Deal*, is a shining pathway. *Get Published* truly is a complete guide. Laura Cross has done most of the research for you. Like the story of Theseus and the Minotaur, Ms. Cross's book has left a string leading you through the dark and cold to publication and back again. All the information is here. You just have to plot it out for yourself and use it.

Ms. Cross educates you by explaining how the business works, she defines book categories and terminology, gives you the skinny on what agents can do, what they want, and where to find representation; she walks you through marketing, how to create a platform, select agents, offers tips on creating pitches and queries, how to put-together a nonfiction book proposal, along with information on how a book sells and all the way up to contracts, including advice from published authors and what worked for them. It is very thorough. The dos and don'ts that pepper the book are worth the cost of the book alone.

Ms. Cross has written in a voice that is instructive, encouraging, and inspirational. In *Get Published* writers will find valuable information to help them on their path toward becoming a career author.

Andrea Campbell,
Author and teacher

* * *

Andrea Campbell is the author of twelve nonfiction books on a variety of topics including forensic science, criminal law, and entertaining. She is currently writing a historical-biography that will be released in June 2010 through Overlook Press. You can visit Andrea at her website: **www.andreacampbell.com**.

Introduction

Congratulations. You have a compelling nonfiction book idea. All you need now is to land the book deal.

A literary agent helps you do just that. Agents review thousands of queries each year searching for talented writers and material to present to publishers. Literary agents sell between 80 and 90 percent of books to publishers. You have a much better chance of getting a book deal when you have an agent representing you to publishers.

Acquiring an agent can be easy. All you need to do is develop a marketable book idea, and follow the literary agency's submission guidelines to be considered for representation.

This book will teach you how to:
- Establish your author platform
- Find a literary agent
- Select an agent that is right for you
- Put together an effective pitch package to attract an agent
- Craft a query letter
- Prepare a book proposal
- Protect yourself from scams
- Evaluate and understand agency contracts
- Maintain a positive working relationship with your agent

Throughout the book you will find step-by-step instructions on how to complete the necessary tasks along with expert tips from reputable agents. "How I Acquired My Agent" sections showcase an author who successfully hired a literary agent and reveals the techniques used to acquire the agent.

Section I covers the planning, preparation, and research necessary for acquiring a literary agent.

Section II shows you how to create all the essential elements of a pitch package, including the query letter, and book proposal, and how to successfully submit your work for consideration.

Section III leads you along the final path of your journey to acquiring an agent and becoming a published author by giving you tips on how to evaluate an offer and work in harmony with your agent to sell your book.

SECTION I:

PREPARING TO
ACQUIRE A LITERARY AGENT

Chapter 1 | Why You Need An Agent

Literary agents are experienced and knowledgeable about the publishing industry. They handle the business responsibilities and aspects of selling your book, and offer many benefits for writers who want to become successful, traditionally published authors.

What Literary Agents Do

For unpublished writers, the book industry can be a competitive and confusing marketplace. A literary agent can help you navigate the landscape and get your foot in the door at a publishing house. Agents are always searching for talented writers. Like matchmakers, they bring authors (the sellers) and publishers (the buyers) together.

A literary agent acts as an author's representative. The agent's job is to find a publishing house to buy your book idea and negotiate the contract and subsidiary rights on your behalf.

A typical day in the life of a literary agent may include:

- Reviewing query letters to acquire new writers
- Corresponding with current author-clients
- Pre-selling books
- Reading book proposals
- Discussing needed edits and rewrites with authors
- Explaining editorial responses and contract details
- Meeting with editors
- Following up on submissions to publishers
- Handling requests for subsidiary rights
- Attending industry conferences
- Keeping current with trade magazines
- Tracking clients' book promotion campaigns

Before joining in partnership, let us explore the buyer — the publishing industry.

The Publishing Industry

As readers' lifestyles change and new technologies emerge, the publishing industry continues to expand and shift. Today, there are numerous options for publishing your book: from traditional commercial publishing with a large or mid-size publishing house to small or regional publishers, or even self-publishing, print-on-demand, or digital publishing.

The diverse publishing industry is made up of:
- Six large publishers
  - Random House
  - Penguin Group
  - Simon & Schuster
  - HarperCollins
  - Hachette Book Group
  - Georg von Holtzbrinck Publishing Group
- Several hundred mid-size publishers
- About 100 university presses
- More than 85,000 small publishers, self-publishers, and subsidy publishers (vanity presses)

How traditional publishing works

For fiction books or narrative nonfiction work, a literary agent will submit a complete manuscript to an editor for consideration. But for prescriptive nonfiction books, the agent will provide a book proposal and sample chapters. The book proposal is analyzed by an editorial review committee, which may consist of editors, production staff, sales representatives, in-house publicists, and even the publisher or owner herself. If a publishing company decides your idea is viable, they will offer you a contract and an advance against future book sales.

Approximately 80 percent of all published books fail to earn back the advance given to the authors, and with the cost to produce an average hardcover book escalating upward of $50,000, publishers consider several factors before committing to develop a book:

- The quality of your writing
- If your idea is marketable
- Your ability to promote and publicize the book
- If the book will be timely when published
- How large the audience is for the book
- If the book has other sales potential, such as film rights
- If your book could be a series or produce spin-offs
- If you can acquire cover quotes and a foreword
- Potential distribution channels
- How many other similar books are on the market
- If major bookstores will stock it

QUICK FACTS:
- 85 percent of new titles published each year are nonfiction
- First-time authors write 75 percent of the new nonfiction books published each year

---

After a traditional publisher has purchased your book, they will:

- **Take editorial control of the content**
  The editor works with the author to prepare the book for publication. Substantive editing is done to ensure the content is arranged appropriately for clarity and flow. Copyediting is performed to correct any errors in formatting, punctuation, spelling, grammar, word tense and usage, and syntax. The text is also checked for copyrights, trademarks, permissions, citations, and libel. The editor will also register the copyright and obtain an ISBN (International Standard Book Number) and

Library of Congress Control Number.

- **Design the book cover and sales copy**
  The graphic department will prepare the artwork, layout the cover elements, and select the typefaces. The marketing department writes the sales copy and selects testimonials and review quotes for inclusion on the back cover and dust-jacket flaps.

- **Prepare the book for printing**
  The art department designs the interior layout, typesets the text, and creates the necessary graphics, such as charts, maps, and illustrations. A galley is prepared for final review and proofing.

- **Print the book**
  This process involves selecting and ordering the paper, scheduling the press, making the plates, folding and trimming the printed press sheets and sewing or gluing them into the book's spine.

- **Prepare promotional material**
  The marketing staff designs and distributes sales aids like posters, signs, fliers, and bookmarks. They also write cover letters to book reviewers and create advertising copy.

- **Market the book**
  Copies of the book are sent to reviewers, advertising space is secured in magazines and online, book tours and media interviews may be organized, and catalogs are created to pre-sell the book to book-dealers.

- **Handle distribution**
  Fulfill orders to major dealers, stores, and libraries.

- **Store returns**
  An average of 20 percent of books shipped to dealers are
  returned to publishers who then store the books in
  warehouses. Returned books are usually sold at a discount.

The Benefits of a Literary Agent

Why not simply bypass the literary agent and approach publishers
directly with your book idea? Acquiring a literary agent as your
representative provides many benefits.

- **An agent understands which editors would be interested in
  your work**
  Agents continually cultivate relationships with publishing
  house editors. They know which editors will be most
  interested in your genre, platform, and writing style based on
  their tastes and needs. They will submit your work to the
  appropriate publishers, the right imprints, the maximum
  number of imprints, and the correct people within those
  imprints – increasing your chances of being published.

- **Agents are aware of changes in the industry**
  The publishing industry is constantly changing. An agent stays
  aware of shifts in new media and markets to better navigate
  the obstacles and opportunities for first-time authors.

- **Editors prefer agent submissions**
  Agents have more influence with a publisher than an unknown
  writer does. If an agent has pre-screened the material and is
  willing to represent an author's work, an editor considers it
  more worthy than if it is submitted directly by a writer.

- **Agents ensure your book proposal is read**
  Most large publishing houses only accept submissions from
  agents. An agent will work with you to make sure your

material is as strong as it can be before submitting it for
consideration.

- **An agent can ensure a better deal and create a bidding war**
  Agents will get your book proposal seen by the maximum
  number of publishers. If multiple publishers are interested in
  the project, a powerful agent can coordinate a bidding war.
  Without an agent you will not know what other publishers
  may offer.

- **Agents understand publishing contracts and are experienced
  negotiators**
  Publishing contracts are written for the benefit of the
  publishing house, not the writer. An agent is familiar with
  contractual language and can negotiate a contract that is
  beneficial to the author, ensuring larger advances and
  royalties and changing smaller contract points to your favor. A
  good agent will arrange for an escalator clause to be included
  in your contract, which provides a bonus payment should your
  book accomplish a specific feat, such as making a bestseller
  list or being picked up by a book-of-the-month club. Without
  an agent, you have no leverage to negotiate better terms.

- **An agent acts as a buffer**
  The publishing industry is a business. An agent acts as buffer
  between you and the business issues so you can maintain a
  creative relationship with your editor and focus on writing.
  Agents deal with rejection letters, so you do not have to think
  about them. Agents track payments and ensure you are paid
  on schedule. An agent also handles publicity, marketing, and
  legal aspects of your career and can offer guidance as business
  issues arise.

- **An agent will ensure you receive better subsidiary rights**
  Subsidiary rights are secondary rights that can be sold with a

book. They include translation rights, audio rights, film rights, book club rights, serial rights, foreign rights, and additional rights. Agents negotiate to retain some of these rights and take responsibility for selling them on your behalf: responding to inquiries, sending out books, handling paperwork, and arranging deals. Successful agents use co-agents in Hollywood to try to sell the movie and television rights for your book, creating additional revenue and royalties Without an agent, the publisher will often retain these rights. (Television and movie rights for prescriptive nonfiction books have become more frequent in recent years, with the optioning of books such as *What To Expect When You're Expecting* and *He's Just Not That Into You*.)

- **An agent has contacts to help your career**
An agent's network can help you land endorsements and forewords from other authors and experts, publicity tie-ins, teaching engagements, speaking opportunities, and media coverage, and more writing assignments.

- **An agent is your advocate**
Editors may have 30 titles to edit each year and are forced to prioritize them. Titles with agents take priority at publishing houses and receive more attention from editors than books without agent representation. Agents will advocate for quality book cover designs, higher marketing budgets, and better placement. If an editor leaves the company, an agent will work to ensure the new editor assigned to your book is enthusiastic about it being published. Without an agent, if your editor leaves, you and your project will be orphaned. If your first book under-performs and your publisher drops you, your agent has a vested interest in finding another publisher for you. Without an agent, if your first book is not successful, you will have a difficult time finding another agent or publisher for

subsequent books. Your agent may be the only stable element of your writing career.

How To Know When You Are Ready for an Agent

Now that you understand what a literary agent can do for you and have decided to acquire one, how do you know when you are ready for an agent? Below are questions to consider:

Have you explored all options for publishing your book?

Agents only sell to large and mid-size publishers, so your first task is to determine if traditional publishing with a large publishing house is the best option for your book. If you write poetry, short story collections, academic books, or specialized nonfiction, or if your writing focuses on a specific area, such as Bed and Breakfast Inns of Maine, you may fare better approaching small publishers directly. If you wish to retain complete control of your project, then you might choose to self-publish your work and forego hiring an agent to sell your book to a traditional publisher.

Have you researched agents and created an agent file?

Individual agents within each literary agency represent specific types of books. If you approach an agent who does not consider your particular genre, you have wasted your time submitting a pitch. A well-researched and focused approach will help you acquire the right agent more quickly. Chapter 4 details how to find and research agents, and teaches you how to create an effective agent file based on your specific needs.

Do you have a pitch package?

An agent expects you to know the selling points of your book and be able to convey them effectively with your pitch package. For nonfiction writers, your pitch package is made up of a query letter, book proposal, and two to three sample chapters. Chapter 5 outlines the essential requirements of a pitch package.

Is your book proposal polished?

Your book proposal should be professionally edited, proofread, and critiqued to ensure it is the best it can be. It needs to be polished and provide a complete picture of the finished work. Chapter 7 shows you how to create the book proposal.

Is your book idea marketable?

A key component to acquiring an agent and publishing deal is a marketable product. Below are questions you can answer to determine the marketability of your idea to an agent.

1. **Does a nearly identical book already exist?**
    If a book already exists that is almost identical to your idea you will have trouble selling yours to an agent or publisher. You will need to ensure and show an agent how your book will be better than the ones already on the market.

2. **How large is the potential audience for your book?**
    Who will buy your book? If only you and a handful of readers are interested in your book's subject, a publisher or agent will not be begging for your manuscript. A valuable resource for determining how many potential readers there are for your subject matter is to browse the sales ranks of similar books on the market and review the bestseller lists in your genre. *Publishers Weekly* magazine (**www.publishersweekly.com**) provides bestseller lists, and columns on "Retail Sales" and "Trends and Topics" that you may find helpful. *The New York Times* book review section (**www.nytimes.com/pages/books**) also lists bestsellers by category. The Website Titlez (**www.titlez.com**) allows you to track Amazon.com sales rank history by keyword, title, or author and compare similar books by genre or title.

3. **Does your book have series potential?**
    Spin-off or series potential is not mandatory to sell your book

idea, but an agent or publisher is more interested in projects that begat more product. Books with spin-off or series potential are considered more valuable.

Do you have a platform and strong promotion plan?
Agents and publishers prefer authors who have an established platform. Your ability to promote your book will be vital for acquiring an agent and a book deal. Chapter 3 outlines how to establish and grow your author platform.

Have you mapped out a writing career?
Agents represent writing careers, not authors who write only one book. They look for authors who have a vision and plan for their writing careers. Before approaching an agent you should have a clear understanding of what you want to accomplish with your writing and the next step along your path as an author.

Checklist for Nonfiction Writers
- ✓ Agent file
- ✓ Query letter
- ✓ Book proposal
- ✓ Sample chapters
- ✓ Marketable idea
- ✓ Author platform and promotional plan
- ✓ Career map

How I Acquired My Agent: David Meerman Scott

Website - **www.davidmeermanscott.com**
Blog - **www.webinknow.com**
Twitter - **http://twitter.com/dmscott**

Books: *The New Rules of Marketing and PR: How to Use News Releases, Blogs, Viral Marketing and Online Media to Reach Buyers Directly* (2007, John Wiley & Sons, Inc.), *World Wide Rave: Creating Triggers that Get Millions of People to Spread Your Ideas and Share Your Stories* (2009, John Wiley & Sons, Inc.)
Genre: Nonfiction (business)
Agent: Bill Gladstone, Waterside Productions

I wrote a free eBook in January 2006 and released it on my blog. The free eBook became an immediate hit. Dozens of bloggers linked to it within days and it had 50,000 downloads in the first month. I wanted to expand the ideas into a business book and on the recommendation of a friend; I contacted Bill Gladstone at Waterside Productions.

My pitch was very simple, I told Bill that I had 50,000 downloads of my free eBook in a month and that many bloggers were talking up my ideas. He signed me immediately.

We worked on a proposal together and sold the book to John Wiley and Sons, Inc. *The New Rules of Marketing and PR: How to Use News Releases, Blogs, Podcasting, Viral Marketing and Online Media to Reach Buyers Directly* came out in hardcover in June 2007. The paperback edition was released in January 2009 and a second edition is scheduled for March 2010. The book spent many months on the BusinessWeek bestseller list and is now published in 24 languages.

Since then, I have also published *World Wide Rave: Creating*

Triggers that Get Millions of People to Spread Your Ideas and Share Your Stories, also with Wiley and with Bill as the agent.

What I have learned from this experience and through many discussions with other authors and publishers is that in order to get a business book published, you need to prove to agents and publishers that your book will sell. One of the best ways to do that is to show, through your Web content (eBooks, blog, YouTube videos, and so on) that you are popular and will sell books. My recommendation for those who want to publish a business book is to focus attention on building an online platform. Without one, you are unlikely to attract the attention of agents and publishers.

Chapter 2 | Understanding the Market

To acquire an agent, it is important to know what is happening in the market, where you fit in, and what agents want. The more understanding you have, the better you can position yourself.

What Agents Look For

The overwhelming majority of material agents receive is un-publishable or poorly presented. Literary agents say they accept 1 percent of submissions. They reject the other 99 percent of submissions because:

1. The material is poorly written, and/or
2. The agent does not think they can sell it

FAST FACTS
87 % is considered amateurish and un-publishable
4 % is considered quality material but it lacks a target market
4 % is considered good writing but the market for it is already saturated
3 % has a potential market but is poorly written or researched
1 % is considered potentially good material if the writing is revised and polished
1 % is considered well written and ready to be presented to a publisher

---

With their understanding of what publishers are looking for, agents consider these factors prior to representing an author's work:

- The quality of your writing
- The marketability of the book
- Potential for subsidiary rights
- Your author platform
- Your potential writing career

The quality of your writing

Agents want original, well-written, and non-derivative works. A writer's understanding of their genre as well as their reader's expectations is essential to produce quality material. (See the section below on Understanding Your Genre for tips.)

For nonfiction, agents look for:
- A structure that flows logically and leads the reader to a specific goal
- Writing that delivers help to solve a problem or make one's life better

The marketability of the book

Agents consider how many readers the book will attract. If you can identify a large, specific group of potential readers who want or need what you plan to write about you will increase your chances of snagging an agent and a book deal.

If the market could already be saturated - such as books on the next best diet, unless you can prove that your idea is unique and that you have an established network of readers, your agent will consider it a hard sell and take a pass. Agents may also consider whether a book will tie in with current events that will help sell it to readers.

Potential for subsidiary rights

Subsidiary rights present a potential bounty of revenue for an author, and hence, an author's agent. If your book has the possibility to be serialized, made into a film or television movie, become a book-of-the-month club selection, or merchandised in other ways, an agent will weigh this information when considering you as a client.

Your author platform

Agents expect nonfiction authors to have an established platform before approaching them for representation. In particular, agents say they look for a strong Web presence including a Website or blog and social media networking that builds the writer's readership base. If a book is synergistic with an author's brand, an agent sees potential for additional promotion, publicity, and sales.

Your potential writing career

For a literary agent, investing in a writer requires a commitment of time and resources, and the agent's reputation. The agent wants to ensure his or her commitment is worth the effort by investing in an author who will have a career in writing; an author who will produce more than one book and will be passionate about promoting and sustaining their writing career.

Publishing Trends

If you attend writer's conferences, read writing magazines, or subscribe to industry newsletter or blogs, you are bound to hear predictions from the 'experts' that *this* type of writing is in and *that* type of book is out. Such pronouncements should not interfere with your primary goal, which is to write an exceptional book proposal and acquire an agent to sell your book. Know the market, but do not worry about the market.

Popular trends

Whenever a book becomes a bestseller, publishers and readers look for more of the same. When *Marley and Me* became a hit, publishers released similar books about dogs and their owners, and readers devoured them – for a while. Eventually, the market becomes saturated and readers grow tired of reading the same story or subject matter.

Publishing trends come and go. A popular topic today will be different a year from now. For that reason, it is best to be aware of trends but do not write to trends. Focus your writing on your expertise. You must be invested in and passionate about your subject. Otherwise, you will not be able to convey enthusiasm to an agent, publisher or reader.

Timeliness and relevance

If your topic is timely and relevant, agents will consider that aspect of your idea when considering representing it. Following a current 'popular trend' is not advised but being aware of lifestyle shifts and readers' needs may benefit your book's potential sales.

Think about ways your book may be tied to current events and book sales. The economic downturn, concern for the environment and depletion of natural resources, and an aging generation of baby-boomers are just three major elements affecting readers' lifestyles.

As baby boomers age, they are planning for their parents' medical and caretaker needs and focusing on staying healthy and in-shape. The financial crisis that began in 2007 has lead to many people looking for unique ways to find jobs, repair their credit and create debt strategies, avoid foreclosure, and create new streams of revenue, which leads to an increase in entrepreneurship and a need for books on running and marketing small businesses.

Many readers are looking for ways to save money by doing their own repairs and home improvements, which creates a rise in do-it-yourself-book sales, or lowering their budgets by vacationing close to home, leading to an increase in sales of regional and local travel books. Environmental concern has created an enormous opportunity for 'green' books.

Some books are tied to the calendar. Everything from the twentieth anniversary in 2009 of the Tiananmen Square uprising, to the thirtieth anniversary in 2007 of the release of the film "Star Wars" can create reader interest in a specific subject. In 2009, readers saw the release of a plethora of historical books commemorating the bicentennial of Abraham Lincoln's birth.

Understanding Your Genre

Genre is a set of criteria for a category of composition. A book's genre helps inform a potential reader what to expect emotionally, structurally, and intellectually. Genre, then, creates a set of expectations and it is your job as the writer to know what those expectations are and deliver them to the reader. Bookstores categorize books by genre making it easy for readers to find the type of books they enjoy. Understanding your genre also assists you in marketing your book idea effectively.

Nonfiction

Nonfiction books stand or fall on the delivery of the promise to help the reader. Regardless of your genre, as a nonfiction writer, you either:

1. Help the reader fix a problem; usually self-help, how-to, reference, inspirational, travel guides, and cookbooks serve this purpose.

2. Provide information to expand a reader's knowledge and worldview; this is the intent of most narrative nonfiction works and includes memoirs, biographies, autobiographies, historical accounts, and books on current events.

The most effective way to understand nonfiction genre is to peruse complementary, as well as competitive, books in the same genre as your book idea. Analyze the books in your niche and note:

- The layout - Do most contain sidebars, case studies, anecdotes, photos or charts?

- The structure – The number of chapters and sections, and the overall book length.

- The delivery - Is the style casual or formal: is the tone fun and motivational, or sincere and cautionary?

- The content – Is the manuscript packed with hard-hitting information, statistical/technical overload, complex theories, or detailed historical accounts? Or, does it contain simple step-by-step instructions, homespun advice, basic processes, or easily understood philosophy?

- The purpose – Is it to educate, motivate, expose, entertain, convince, inspire, or connect and share the human experience?

How-To
How-to books outsell every other nonfiction genre. Within the how-to niche the bestselling categories are: Business/Leadership, Parenting, Sex, Money/Finances/Investing, Dieting/Weight Loss, and Health/Fitness. How-to books are filled with instructions, valuable information, tips, suggestions, examples, and illustrations. Information is presented sequentially with each chapter supporting the overall concept. These books conclude with the reader achieving the "goal."

Books: *Starting on a Shoestring: Building a Business without a Bankroll* by Arnold S. Goldstein, *Scrapbook Basics* by Michele Gebrandt, and *WordPress for Dummies* by Lisa Sabin-Wilson.

Self-Help
Self-Help books encompass the realm of psychology, advice, and personal growth. The most popular category is Relationships. Self-help books have more examples than how-to books. The author's style is casual, as if conversing with an old friend across the table.

Books: *Surviving the Breakup* by Judith S. Wallerstein and Joan B. Kelly, *From Panic to Power* by Lucinda Bassett, and *Overcoming Depression* by Demetri Papolos.

Travel Guides
Travel guidebooks are always in demand, especially if they cover a location that has not been saturated or take a fresh spin on a topic, such as *The Top 100 Romantic Places to Kiss*. Travel guides require detailed research and must provide all the necessary information and tips to help the reader successfully plan a trip to the destination.

Books: *Away for the Weekend* by Eleanor Berman, and *Europe on $5 a Day* by Arthur Frommer.

Cooking and Food
Hundreds of new cookbooks are published each year. To succeed in this competitive genre you need a distinctive theme that captures the reader's attention. Cookbooks incorporate vibrant photos, systematic detailed instructions, and a casual 'you-can-do-it' style.

Books: *Almost Vegetarian* by Diana Shaw, *The Complete Book of Bread Machine Baking* by Kristi Fuller, and *The Santa Monica Farmer's Market Cookbook* by Amelia Saltsman.

Inspirational/Religious/Spiritual/Metaphysical
Religious, inspirational, and spiritual books share themes of a particular belief system and provide wisdom, motivation, and

advice to guide readers to live a full life in harmony with specific concepts. Metaphysical books investigate principles of reality that transcend science, such as astrology, numerology, and psychic ability. These books uplift readers' spirits and require an author who is closely attuned to the readership: who they are, what they assume, and their "language." The writer must have a full understanding of the history of the subject.

Books: *The Purpose-Driven Life* by Rick Warren, *Conversations with God* by Neale Donald Walsch, and *The Case for Faith* by Lee Strobel.

Reference

A reference book contains authoritative facts. Successful reference books never go out-of-date. Authors can simply update the content every five to eight years. Popular reference categories include Computer and Internet books as well as Directories. "Coffee table" books also fall under this genre and Architecture, Art, and Photography are popular subgenres.

Books: *The Quotable Star Wars* by Stephen J. Sansweet, *The Big Book of 60,000 Baby Names* by Diane Stafford, and *The 21st Century Crossword Puzzle Dictionary* by Kevin McCann and Mark Diehl.

Humor

Humor books are filled with content that is witty and entertaining. They are usually given as gifts. They are short, funny, and have an identifiable audience, such as cat owners, golfers, or parents.

Books: *If Dogs Could Talk* by Joel Zadak, *The Women's Daily Irony Supplement* by Judy Gruen, and *Unusually Stupid Americans* by Ross and Kathryn Petras.

Medical and Science
Medical and science books enlighten and educate readers about the medical and scientific fields. They can be successful sellers. They require extensive research, interviewing and fact checking. They incorporate charts, graphs, illustrations, and a thorough glossary.

Books: *A Brief History of Time* by Stephen Hawking, and *The Physics of Star Trek* by Lawrence M. Krauss.

Narrative nonfiction
Narrative nonfiction, also referred to as creative nonfiction, is truthful writing that reads like a novel. It straddles the line between nonfiction and fiction, incorporating storytelling techniques such as plot, conflict, and dialogue. Narrative nonfiction requires:

1. Factual subject matter
2. Exhaustive research
3. Compelling narrative or a literary prose style

History
History books have a scholarly tone and are often written by experts - not necessarily a professional historian, but at least someone who has extensively studied the subject. Historical stories are compelling to readers when they evoke a sense of place by maintaining the customs, culture, and knowledge of the period, as well as providing relevance to our lives today, or revealing something new about a well-known, or little-known, event. Military books are considered a sub-genre of history.

Popular books and authors: *Killing Pablo* and *Black Hawk Down* by Mark Bowden, *Band of Brothers* by Stephen E. Ambrose, *1776* by David McCullough, *How The Irish Saved Civilization* by Thomas Cahill, and *Seabiscuit* by Laura Hillenbrand.

Adventure
Adventure books consist of a man-against-nature story. They have an extreme and dramatic quality and are set in an exotic location.

Popular books and authors: *Into the Wild* and *Into Thin Air* by Jon Krakauer, and *The Perfect Storm* by Sebastian Junger.

Travelogues
Travelogues incorporate the author's travel experience and may include travel guide details about the destination.

Popular books and authors: *A Walk in the Woods* and *In a Sunburned Country* by Bill Bryson, and *Under The Tuscan Sun* by Frances Mayes.

Biography
Along with extensive research and minute fact verification, biographies require the author to be devoted to the subject matter but objective enough to go wherever the truth may lead in order to create an accurate portrayal. Biographies come with their own set of challenges, such as:

- Will the subject (if alive) or the family cooperate with the telling of his or her story?
- How will 'fans' of the subject respond to negative revelations?
- Has the subject been covered thoroughly or do you have a new perspective or theory to present to readers?
- Does the subject warrant cradle-to-grave coverage or is there one inspirational event or portion of your subject's life worthy of exploration?

Popular books and authors: *John Adams* by David McCullough, *JFK* by James W. Douglass, and *The Snowball: Warren Buffett and the Business of Life* by Alice Schroeder.

Memoir

The challenge of memoir is to write a personal account, whether tragic or inspiring, that has a universal connection. Memoir must transcend the personal and become a shared experience for readers.

Popular books and authors: *Angela's Ashes* by Frank McCourt, *Running with Scissors* by Augusten Burroughs, and *Dreams of My Father* by Barack Obama.

True Crime

True Crime accounts incorporate the art of the newspaper reporter. It requires investigative, analytical attention to detail and some understanding of police and forensic procedures. The author must present an in-depth study of the cast of characters, the victim's family, the detectives, the lawyers, and the perpetrator, and effectively capture and convey what is identifiable and intriguing.

Popular books and authors: *In Cold Blood* by Truman Capote, *And The Sea Will Tell* by Vincent Bugliosi, *The Stranger Beside Me* by Ann Rule, *The Devil In The White City* by Erik Larson, *Echoes in the Darkness* by Joseph Wambaugh, and *The Executioner's Song* by Norman Mailer.

Chapter 3 | Establishing Your Platform

As a nonfiction writer, you must have an established platform. Without one, you will not land a book deal, and you will not acquire an agent. There are no exceptions to this publishing industry rule. No matter how outstanding the content may be, an author platform is essential to sell your book. A publisher will not commit to signing an author and releasing a book unless they know the writer has a large following of potential readers. A writer seeking an agent for commercial publication cannot ignore this fact.

Establishing Your Platform

A platform encompasses the ways you are visible and attracting potential readers. It conveys your expertise and influence. If you are recognized as a leader on a specific topic then you have attained a successful platform. A platform requires substantial effort and time to build reputation, credibility, and an extensive following. At the minimum, you will need to invest a year in developing your platform before pitching a nonfiction book idea to an agent.

Platforms that impress agents and publishers:
- Speaking in front of 50,000 people per year (either all at one time or divided into several speaking engagements.)
- Repeat expert guest segments on national television.
- A subscriber list of at least 30,000 potential readers.
- A video on YouTube that receives more than 1 million hits.
- Weekly guest appearances on a national radio show or hosting your own national radio show.
- A daily or weekly column in a national, syndicated newspaper or a monthly column in a magazine with wide circulation.

Platform Building Strategies

Here are ways to establish a solid platform:

Develop and promote your expertise

Expertise includes your knowledge on a particular topic and how well others regard you. You must earn the respect and trust of others to be considered a credible expert. This is developed through experience in the field, testimonials, endorsements, speaking engagements, and teaching your skills to others.

Create a Website

Every potential author needs a Website. This is your home base on the Internet where you can place excerpts from your forthcoming book, photo headshots, contact information, videos, and links to your Facebook and Twitter profiles. If you already have a Website when you begin approaching media you will have an edge over other writers.

Brand yourself

Establish an author identity and use it consistently throughout your material. Your personal brand is how you package and present yourself to readers to distinguish and differentiate yourself from other writers.

Set up a blog

The wider your Web presence the better. A blog adds to your credibility, helps you establish your expertise, and provides a means to capture potential readers for your database. Make a writing plan and consistently post to your blog. You should write about your expertise on your niche topic. Comment on other author's blogs and write guest posts to continue to increase traffic to your site.

Create a video
Posting a video on your Website or blog substantially increases traffic. It also shows potential media outlets how you will perform on television and radio. Be sure to post your video on YouTube (**www.youtube.com**) as well. Visitors to YouTube search for videos the way users of search engines seek keywords. You can shoot a video related to your niche or a trailer for your book.

Social networking
Social networking is a powerful marketing tool. Facebook (**www.facebook.com**), Twitter (**http://twitter.com**), LinkedIn (**www.linkedin.com**), RedRoom (**www.redroom.com**), and other online networking sites give you access to connections and a platform to share your writing and expertise.

Gather endorsements
Recommendations from successful authors and well-known industry leaders are a potent sales tool. Ask your connections if they can provide testimonials or endorsements of your.

Podcasts
Hosting a weekly syndicated audio recording or podcast can introduce you to a wide audience of followers. The segments can also be presented to radio programmers to show your potential as a guest on one of their shows. Podcasts can be based on topics within your specialized niche of expertise.

Podcasts can be created using free software available from Audacity (**http://audacity.sourceforge.net**) and syndicated through iTunes (**www.itunes.com**).

Newsletters
Your Website and blog should include an opt-in page to capture subscribers and potential readers of your upcoming book. Stay in contact with your subscribers with a weekly e-zine or newsletter

that provides valuable content they have shown an interest in reading. Services such as ConstantContact (**www.constantcontact.com**), Aweber (**www.aweber.com**), and 1ShoppingCart (**www.1ShoppingCart.com**) make it easy and affordable to create a customized newsletter, e-mail it to your subscribers, and manage your subscriptions.

Offer excerpts

Posting excerpts from your forthcoming book on your website or blog encourages reader interest and establishes trust and loyalty. Consider giving away an eBook or mini-book of writings to entice visitors to sign-up and be added to your database.

Create a media kit

Make it easy for journalists and TV reporters to use you as a source for interviews by putting an online media kit on your Website. Your media kit can include photos/headshots, a list of topics you speak on, sample interview questions, a portfolio of media clips, a backgrounder or bio, excerpts from you book, a calendar of upcoming events or speaking engagements, and press releases.

Write articles

Approach magazines and news outlets that would be receptive to an article, op-ed, or column on your niche topic. Write articles on your area of expertise and distribute them on article syndication sites such as EzineArticles (**www.ezinearticles.com**) and document sharing sites including Scribd (**www.scribd.com**). Be sure to include a link to your Website, blog, and other media outlets in the signature.

Distribute a news release

An online news release has the potential to garner a wide range of media opportunities. A news release is similar to a press release. It is a one page presentation of newsworthy information of interest to reporters and news agencies. Find a way to tie your expertise to a current event. If your niche is social media marketing and a new study is about to be published that indicates the majority of corporate America now utilizes social media to market their products and services, write a news release stating that information, and align it to your expertise. Conclude with a brief synopsis of your background and include contact information and a link to your online media page.

You can use a news distribution service to disseminate your release. Major U.S. news distribution services include: Business Wire (**www.businesswire.com**), PR Newswire (**www.prnewswire.com**), and PRWeb (**www.prweb.com**). Their services range in price from $200 to $800.

Teach

Turn your topic into a class, workshop, or seminar to attract an audience interested in your subject. Teaching also shows agents and editors your ability to effectively convey ideas. Consider approaching conferences, associations, universities, community colleges, lifelong learning programs, community organizations, or adult education centers to begin teaching. Then transfer your in-person teaching success to online classes and reach an even broader range of potential customers.

Speaking engagements

Opportunities to speak are abundant. Depending on your area of expertise, you may consider approaching corporations, universities, events, or major conferences. If you can line up a network of large venues for speaking engagements it will strongly support your author platform when searching for an agent and publisher. Consider hiring a speaking agent to book bigger engagements.

Radio and television
Send your media kit to local radio and television stations that would be a good fit for your topic. Once you have garnered a few local programs, expand your reach to regional and national platforms.

Magazines and newspapers
Present yourself as a potential expert source to magazine writers and newspaper columnists, using:
- Help A Reporter Out (**www.HelpAReporterOut.com)**
- Reporter Connection (**www.ReporterConnection.com**)
- Pitch Rate (**www.PitchRate.com**)

Expert Advice: Literary Agent Barbara Poelle

Irene Goodman Literary Agency
27 West 24th Street, Suite 700B
New York, New York 10010
www.irenegoodman.com
queries@irenegoodman.com

On how to find an agent: You find an agent the same way you would write a book: research, research, and research. There are so many viable sources in every media these days that a big red flag starts waving if you are sending me a children's book when my profile clearly states I am looking for humorous nonfiction. I probably can't trust your work to have much attention to detail.

On what makes a good query letter: Three things: The Hook, The Book and The Cook. You should be able to tell me about your book in a succinct sentence - this is the "hook". Then you should expand the description into five or six sentences - which is the "book" - and can also be used as an "elevator pitch," meaning a verbal pitch when meeting agents, editors, and the basic public face to face. And finally, the "cook" - which is you, and it doesn't matter if you have zero publishing credits - just be able to state in the cook section <u>why this book</u>, <u>why you</u> and <u>why now</u>.

On what she looks for in nonfiction book proposals: I'm looking for Platform. How many people are already excited about a book by you? I wish I could tell you that a good story or an interesting topic will always thunder across the finish line victorious, but in today's media driven world, there must be evidence of staying power; having a solid online presence or growing multi-media platform is like stapling a golden ticket to the proposal.

On paying attention to trends: I say treat your book the way you live: with 98 percent passion and 2 percent common sense. Pay attention to trends but write what you're passionate about.

Query letter mistakes to avoid: The mistakes people make in queries are so numerous and hilarious that they themselves could make up an entire book. (Hmm, now there's an idea, anybody know an agent?) Poorly executed queries vary from misinformed to outright insulting and before we went electronic, they might also arrive with "gifts" ranging from homemade food products to bedazzled soda cozies.

Tips for maintaining a good working relationship: Like any relationship, respect is the cornerstone. There needs to be a great deal of trust and enthusiasm on both sides of the table, but above all, the understanding that this is a business venture and everybody wants the results to be wildly successful. I absolutely adore my clients; I find them to be as delightfully different as their genres, but what they all have in common is a great deal of focus and patience in an industry that demands both.

How I Acquired My Agent: Laurie Pawlik-Kienlen

Website: **http://theadventurouswriter.com**
Blogs: **http://theadventurouswriter.com/blogwriting**,
http://theadventurouswriter.com/blog,
http://theadventurouswriter.com/blogbaby,
and **http://seejanesoar.theadventurouswriter.com**

Books: *See Jane Soar* (awaiting sale to a publisher)
Genre: Nonfiction, health, self-help, inspirational
Agent: Jon Sternfeld, Irene Goodman Literary Agency

I approached a couple dozen publishing houses on my own, and found that it was too time consuming and energy draining. I would rather be writing and blogging than looking for a publisher, and I knew an agent could knock on the doors behind gates I could not get through.

I prepared an airtight book proposal with a strong hook and a well-thought-out idea, and polished it until it sparkled. I built a platform writing nonfiction articles for magazines such as *Reader's Digest, Health, Woman's Day,* and *More*. I am also the Psychology Feature Writer for Suite101, and I created and maintain four blogs. Then I crafted a catchy query to grab an agent's attention.

I researched agents. I looked at the *2009 Guide to Literary Agents*, explored Preditors & Editors, and used a search engine to find "literary agents in America." I queried 14 of the "highly recommended" agents listed on Preditors & Editors and followed the submission guidelines. The agents' Websites I visited had clear submission guidelines, and I took them seriously. The first agent I spoke to told me he could not believe how unprepared and unprofessional writers can be. That made me realize how important it is to thoroughly edit my queries and proposals.

I was tempted to sign on with the first agent I talked to, but he suggested a fairly significant change to my book. He sent the contract and left the ball in my court. Ultimately, I decided not to play with him. It is important to interview your agent like you would interview an employee or colleague. Just because an agent offers to represent you does not mean you are a good fit.

Then Sternfeld contacted me to request my book proposal. Less than a week after I sent it we scheduled a telephone conversation. He was thrilled with my book proposal. "Even if you do not sign with me," he said, "do not change anything. It is great the way it is." We are now in the process of trying to sell it to a publisher.

Chapter 4 | Finding and Selecting an Agent

Finding and selecting an agent that is the right fit for you and your book is essential for the long-term success of your writing career. It involves extensive research and careful consideration.

How to Find Agents

There are many avenues available to find a literary agent. Most authors utilize several resources to locate potential agents.

Referrals

Referrals are the best avenue for finding and contacting an agent. Agents respect and value referrals from an editor, author-client, bookseller, writing expert, or another agent. Ask your associates, friends and network if they can refer you to an agent.

Conferences and literary events

Conferences, seminars, retreats, book festivals, and workshops provide an opportunity to meet an agent in person. Agents expect writers to approach them at these events. Some conferences even schedule sessions for authors to pitch to agents. The goal is to connect with agents and leave them with a positive impression of you and your work for when you submit your pitch package in the future. Some agents may even ask you to send them your book proposal.

Introducing yourself to agents who are a good fit for your writing increases your chances of acquiring an agent; it lays the foundation for a future relationship. The benefits of meeting a literary agent in person are: You create enthusiasm for your project before the agent has even read it; the agent gets an idea of your potential promotion by the way you present yourself and your work; and when you submit your query, it will stand out among the masses of letters they receive daily. Most important, nothing replaces a one-on-one connection and the chemistry it can generate.

Attending conferences and other literary events is a strategy that produces results. Appendix I contains a list of national conferences and additional information about each event. You can follow these ten steps to make the most of your conference experience:

1. Review the conference Website to determine the agents who will be attending or speaking and create a list of the agents you wish to approach.

2. Create a plan of how you will spend your time at the event. Prioritize what you know you *must do* and what you would *like to do if time permits*.

3. Complete your pitch package prior to attending the convention so you will be able to send the material immediately upon returning home from the event.

4. When you arrive at the conference, study the map and the program to better navigate the terrain.

5. Plan to attend both educational and social events, and walk the exhibition floor if one is presented. Collect business cards from everyone you meet.

6. Determine the best time to approach your pre-selected agents – this may be early morning, after a round-table or seminar presentation, or at an opening night cocktail reception.

7. Prepare and practice a pitch speech. Create different versions of your pitch: a 15-second pitch, a one-minute pitch, a two-

minute pitch, and a three-minute pitch. Remember, an agent's time is valuable. Keep your speech simple, exciting, and compelling. Leave the agent with a desire to know more about your project. Pitch the idea first and then follow with your credentials, accomplishments and platform if time allows.

8. Be prepared to answer follow-up questions.

9. Do not ask an agent to read your work or tell him that you will be sending it to his office tomorrow. Wait for an agent to invite you to send your work.

10. As soon as you return home from the conference, send your query letters to the agents who expressed interest. Be sure to mention in the letter that you met them at the conference. Do not send your book proposal unless invited to do so.

Directories

Each year, several literary agent directories are published. Each guide provides detailed information on individual agents, which include the literary agency where the agent works, his contact information, the types of writing he represents, and his submission guidelines. Additional information may also be included such as recent sales, number of annual sales, professional memberships, and total years in business.

Guide to Literary Agents

The *Guide to Literary Agents* is published by Writer's Digest Books and contains a listing of more than 800 literary and script agents. The book provides an index of agents categorized by the genre they represent, which allows you to quickly and conveniently find the agents that represent the type of books you write.

Jeff Herman's Guide to Book Publishers, Editors, & Literary Agents
This directory lists 200 agents who are members of Association of Author's Representatives (AAR), and offers additional details that provide a glimpse of the agents' personalities.

Literary Market Place
Literary Market Place is the most comprehensive directory available. Weighing close to 10 pounds, it has more than 2,000 pages of listings along with a hefty price tag - more than $300. If you have access to a large public library, consider perusing this mammoth guide for free.

The Internet
The array and magnitude of information available via the Internet makes it easier than ever to find literary agents for your book. Forums, blogs, online magazines and directories, and search engines offer an abundance of resources.

Publisher's Lunch (www.publisherslunch.com)
Publisher's Lunch offers a free daily and weekly newsletter that reports on the latest publishing deals and news, including information on the agents involved with the deals and descriptions of the books that sold.

Publisher's Marketplace (www.publishersmarketplace.com)
This Website offers news about the publishing industry as well as a 'Search Members' link to obtain contact information for individual agents and literary agencies, and a listing of the Top 10 Most Visited Agents. The site also offers a paid membership service. For a fee of $20 per month you receive:
- Access to the 'Top Dealmakers' section where you can search by agent, agency or genre and obtain information about recent deals with the specifics of the books and the authors.
- A searchable 'Who Represents' section.

- Links to current industry news from the 'Automat' section, which also includes the tab 'Agencies, Agents, Author Advice', a listing of agent and author blogs.

Publishers Weekly (www.publishersweekly.com)

Publishers Weekly online provides articles about the book industry, includes a "Search" box to obtain information on literary agents and agencies, and presents a weekly "Deals" column with details about major book deals. They also offer *PW Daily*, a free weekly newsletter delivered to your e-mail inbox. You can subscribe to the virtual edition of *Publishers Weekly* magazine for $180 per year to obtain access to more articles, news, and deal listings.

Writer's Market (www.writersmarket.com)

Writer's Market offers a free newsletter that may yield information about literary agents. You can sign up for it on their Website. The site also offers a paid service. For $6 per month you receive online access to the database of agents.

Writer's Digest (www.writersdigest.com)

Writer's Digest's Website is filled with free articles and interviews. They also offer an annual list of the 101 best Websites for writers (**www.writersdigest.com/101bestsites**) and a free e-mail newsletter.

Guide to Literary Agents Blog (www.guidetoliteraryagents.com/blog)

Guide to Literary Agents is an invaluable blog that offers insight into landing an agent. Each week they post an analysis of a pitch in the "Successful Queries" series, interview an agent in the "Agent Advice" column, and publish articles from authors who obtained agents.

Agency Websites
You can easily find the URL for a literary agency by using a search engine and inserting the name of the agency. Agency Websites include a list of clients, recent deals, submission guidelines, and contact information.

Agent Query (www.agentquery.com)
Agent Query provides a free, searchable database of agents and agency information.

QueryTracker (www.querytracker.net)
QueryTracker offers a free list of agents, but the exceptional value of this Website is found in the research they amass and make available. QueryTracker gathers information that is input into their database by authors submitting queries to agents. This information includes the name of the agent who is pitched, the word count of the manuscript, the genre of the book, the date of the response, the type of response, and the final outcome. The collected data reveals important information about specific agents: the overall number of queries sent to each agent and their accept/reject rates, the genre-specific accept/reject history of an agent, and an agent's average response time. For $20 per year, the website also offers even more details about specific agents.

Agent Research (www.agentresearch.com)
This Website offers services ranging in price from free to $360 to access an extensive database with in-depth information about agents.

Writer's Community Sites and Forums
These Websites offer industry information, forum Q&As, and the opportunity to connect with other writers: Red Room, a social media site for writers (**www.redroom.com**); Absolute Write, an online magazine for beginning and professional writers (**www.absolutewrite.com**); AuthorLink, a source on the

publishing world (**www.authorlink.com**); Writing Room, several resources on the art of writing (**www.writingroom.com**); AuthorNation an online community for authors (**www.authornation.com**); and Writing Forums, for creative writing (**www.writingforums.org**).

Agents' Blogs
Agents have their own blogs where they write posts about the publishing industry, their expectations, what they are looking for, their clients' book releases, recent sales, and how to submit a pitch. You can use the Google™ Blog search function to find a listing of literary agent blogs (**http://blogsearch.google.com**).

Popular agent blogs include:
Nathan Bransford (**http://blog.nathanbransford.com**)
Rachelle Gardner (**http://cba-ramblings.blogspot.com**)
Kristin Nelson (**http://pubrants.blogspot.com**)
Jessica Faust (**http://bookendslitagency.blogspot.com**)
Sarah Crowe (**http://acrowesnest.blogspot.com**)
Jennifer Jackson (**http://arcaedia.livejournal.com**)
Jonathon Lyons (**http://lyonsliterary.blogspot.com**)
Lauren MacLeod (**www.strothmanagency.com/articles**)
Holly Root (**http://waxmanagency.wordpress.com**)

Social media
Social media such as LinkedIn, Facebook, and Twitter provide opportunities to expand your networks, grow your contact list, and learn about the publishing industry.

LinkedIn (www.linkedin.com)
When you join groups on LinkedIn you can ask and answer questions and follow discussions on writing, selling, and publishing your book. There are many active writing and publishing groups to consider joining, including:

- Authors, Writers, Publishers, and Agents Group
  Discussions and literary networking for literary agents, writers, publishers, scriptwriters and authors.

- Writing Mafia
  Designed to share information for writers, journalists, copywriters, editors, and authors.

- Writing Professionals
  A group for professional and aspiring novelists, poets, essayists, journalists, editors, and authors.

- Book Publishing Professionals
  An international platform for book publishing professionals to share their expertise and resources. Group includes people involved in book sales, marketing, editorial and production.

- Authors and Publishers Association
  An education and networking group, open to authors, publishers, book manufacturers, agents, publicists, editors, illustrators, graphic designers, ghostwriters, and all others involved in the literary trade.

- Authors, Writers, Publishers, Editors, and Other Professionals
  Group open to all professions within the publishing industry with the goal of connecting, networking, and learning from others in the industry.

- Writing and Editing Professionals
  An international group dedicated to discussing writing and editing.

- Books Sales and Marketing
  Established to provide networking and education on selling and marketing books. This group is for authors, publishers,

editors, book literary agents and future writers.

- Association of Writers
  This group is for anyone interested in writing. Members help one another stay focused and share tips for writing, acquiring and working with an agent, and being published.

Twitter (http://twitter.com)
Twitter is about more than telling your followers what you are doing right now in 140 characters or less. Used effectively, Twitter can garner attention for your writing and platform, and directly connect you with literary agents. Booksquare University (**http://booksquareuniveristy.com**) offers a free directory of hundreds of publishing industry professionals, literary agents, and authors to follow, as well as Tweet Camp, a $399 workshop designed to teach writers how to use Twitter to achieve the best results.

Facebook (www.facebook.com)
Facebook is the most popular social networking site. It is an excellent resource for writers as it allows personal interaction with other members and offers a live feed application to share blog posts, news, links, published articles, and Twitter updates in real time.

The Association of Author's Representatives

The Association of Author's Representatives (AAR) consists of reputable, experienced literary agents. To become a member, agents must have sold 18 books within ten months and adhere to strict ethical guidelines. The AAR Website (**www.AAR-Online.org**) provides a list of members and information on how to contact them.

Identify the literary agent of a book

If you want to know who the agent was for a particular book, examine the acknowledgements page to find the author's agent. Writers tend to thank their literary agents and it is a good way to locate the agent for a specific author. Other ways to identify the literary agent for a book:

- Use a search engine and insert the author's name and "literary agent".

- Use Google™ book search: **www.books.google.com**. In the search box, type in the name of the agent in quotation marks, followed by the word "acknowledgements." Alternatively, type in the name of the book in quotation marks, and then the word "acknowledgements." The search results should lead you to the acknowledgements pages of books listing the searched agent, or in the case of the latter search, the acknowledgements page for the particular book.

- If all else fails, telephone the publisher directly and ask the receptionist for the editor who worked on the book. If you are lucky, you will be transferred to the editor's assistant. Unfortunately, more often than not, your call will be transferred into a sort of telephone limbo zone. If you do reach the editor's assistant, politely request the name of the acting literary agent for the book.

Magazines

You can find the names of literary agents in writer's magazines, such as *The Writer*, *Writer's Digest* and *Poets & Writers*, which publish articles about agents as well as articles written by agents.

Researching Agents

Each agent has different skills, experience, and strengths, and specific types of writing he represents. Prior to approaching and pitching an agent, you need to carefully conduct research to determine which ones are the best fit for your style, personality, needs, and genre. The directories, databases, associations, and Websites listed above will help you collect the information you need to systematically assess prospective agents.

Questions to consider when evaluating an agent:

1. **How important is an agent's experience?**
   An effective agent is one who has established strong contacts with publishers and editors, understands how to negotiate contracts and sell subsidiary rights, and who can work well with writers. Much of this knowledge and skill is acquired through experience. But that does not mean a newer agent is not effective. Many newer agents have a background in editing or book sales, or experience working as assistants to agents. New agents are in the process of building their clientele and are more open to new writers and new ideas, and they have more time to devote to selling books and will work harder to establish sales.

2. **Would you prefer to work with a large, medium, or small agency?**
   Most agencies are small agencies consisting of one or two agents. There are approximately 100 medium-size agencies with three to six people on staff, and 20 large agencies made up of eight or more agents. The prestigious large agencies include: Writers House, William Morris, Curtis Brown, International Creative Management, Janklow & Nesbit, and Sterling Lord Literistic. Large and small agencies offer different benefits.

Large agencies have a full staff: accountants to track payments and disburse funds, attorneys to negotiate contracts, agent assistants to accept your calls when the agent is unavailable, subsidiary rights specialists to sell film, serial, and foreign rights, and publicists to promote your platform. Large agencies focus on commercial properties with additional revenue potential.

Small agencies tend to be more receptive to first-time writers and projects that are less profitable. They are more accessible, easier to reach, and usually respond quicker to queries. You may also find they value and nurture quality relationships with their writer clients.

3. **Does the agent represent nonfiction and does the agent represent your specific sub-category within your genre?**
   Many agents represent either fiction or nonfiction (though some represent both) and specific categories within those genres. Another agent may deal with practical nonfiction, such as business, fitness, and parenting, but not handle narrative nonfiction, such as biography, history, or investigative journalism. It is essential to only approach agents who represent your genre and sub-category. You should have a clear understanding of your type of writing so you do not waste time pitching agents who will not be interested in your book idea.

4. **How many deals has the agent made in her career?**
   An agent who has sold two books has less experience and sales ability than an agent who has sold 200 books. You want an agent that can land you a book deal. Unless the agent is new to the industry and just starting out (and you, therefore, expect her to have a lower number of book sales) then the better choice is the agent who has the higher sales rate.

5. **How many deals has she brokered recently?**
   The publishing industry rewards what you have done lately, not what you have accomplished in the past. You want an agent who is currently active. An agent who has only sold 25 books in her career, but 15 of them were sold in the past year, may be a better choice for representation than an agent who has sold 200 books in her career, but only sold one within the last 12 months.

6. **What kind of publishers has she brokered deals with?**
   Has the agent brokered deals mainly with small publishers or large publishers? Are most of her sales with the same publisher or the same type of publisher, such as academic presses? Ideally you want to work with an agent who brokers most of her sales with major publishers. Major publishers pay higher advances, print more copies of your book, acquire the best distribution, and have larger promotional budgets.

7. **What kinds of advances has she negotiated?**
   Advances vary widely depending on the type of book, which publisher bought it, and the size of the author's platform. Advances range from $5,000 to $500,000. If the agent you are considering consistently acquires advances in the lower range, she may lack experience or negotiating skills.

8. **Do you recognize the authors the agent represents?**
   If you are assessing the viability of a new agent, you may not recognize the names of the authors she represents. But if the agent is well established you should know a few of the writers on her client list.

9. **Are you a good match for the agent's client list?**
   Are the agent's clients synergistic with you and your work? Does she represent books that have a similar subject matter or style as yours? The agent may be a good fit if she

represents a majority of new writers or authors within your same genre. On the other hand, if all the agent's clients are well known, established bestselling authors and you are a first time writer, then she is probably not the right match.

10. **Is the agent receptive to new clients and new writers?**
    You need an agent who is actively looking for new clients. An agent who has been in the business for ten years may not be accepting new clients. As a general rule, a newer agent - one with three or less years of experience - will be more receptive to garnering first-time writers.

Creating an Agent File

Once you have found the agents you are interested in approaching and have sorted through the information, you will need to organize your research. Creating an agent file will help you design a systematic plan to approach your target agents. The goal is to divide and rank your pre-selected list of agents into categories based on your prerequisites, so you can narrow down your options and make informed decisions about the best agents to approach.

You can create your file system with a computer spreadsheet or with simple manila folders. Use as many or as few files and categories as necessary for your particular needs, and order them based on your priorities. For instance, if your goal is to acquire an agent at a large firm, who has less than three years of experience, has sold a minimum of 35 books in his career, most of which were sold in the past 12 months, negotiates strong advances for his clients, is a member of the AAR, and specializes in health and fitness titles – the agents that have most of these characteristics would be filed in your Group 1 folder. You might decide that agents who have most of these qualifications but work in smaller agencies will be filed in your Group 2 folder. You may place agents that meet these requirements but are not yet members of AAR in your Group 3 folder, and so on.

Once you have thoroughly organized your research and prioritized your target agent list, you can effectively and efficiently begin the pitch process. Section II covers what is included in the pitch package, how to successfully create the necessary components, and how to submit your pitch for the best results.

SECTION II:

SUBMITTING THE PITCH

Chapter 5 | The Pitch Package

Now that you have compiled and prioritized your agent file you are ready to begin approaching agents. There are standard procedures and guidelines for pitching agents. The pitch package consists of the query letter and the book proposal. Each component of the pitch package is explained in detail in the following chapters. The query letter is covered in Chapter 6 and the book proposal in Chapter 7. (Below is an overview of each element.)

The query letter
Your initial sales pitch to an agent will be in the form of a one-page query letter. The query letter is your opportunity to grab the agent's attention and motivate him to ask for the book proposal. The goal of the query is to intrigue the agent with your book idea and get him to consider representing you.

The book proposal
The book proposal is a marketing tool used to sell a nonfiction book idea. Publishers commission nonfiction books to be written. In other words, the author does not write the book until *after* a publisher has agreed to publish it. Nonfiction writers land a book deal based on an idea for a book, which is presented in the book proposal, and one to three sample chapters.

Approaching Agents
Acquiring an agent has as much to do with thorough research as it does with approaching a high number of agents. The more agents you approach, the better chance you have of successfully finding an agent. Your agent file should have a minimum of 40 to 50 agents to approach, each ranked in order of their desirability based on your specific requirements.

To make the submission process manageable, you will want to divide your list into groups of eight to ten agents to approach. So if you have a list of 40 agents divided into groups of eight, you will have five groups of agents to approach. Approach your dream agents in Group 1 first. If you do not land an agent in the first round of submissions, do not become discouraged – simply go on to the next set of eight to ten agents to pitch.

Create a file to keep track of when each agent was contacted, when you expect to receive a response, the result of the response, and any follow-up notes. It should not take any longer than four weeks to receive an initial response to your query letter. If you have not received a response from an agent within one month and he is one of your "dream" agents, consider submitting a brief follow-up note. If you still do not receive a response, move on to the next set of agents to query.

Simultaneous submissions

Submitting query letters to more than one agent at the same time is standard practice in the literary world, and it benefits the writer. An agent may take two to four weeks to review your query letter and respond. The response will either be a rejection letter or a request for further material, in which case the agent will need an additional four to eight weeks to review the proposal. If you only query one agent at a time, it could take years to find an agent. Querying multiple agents simultaneously should land you an agent within six months, as long as you are approaching the right agents (which you should be based on your extensive research) and pitching them effectively (which you will be able to do with the knowledge you gained from reading this book.)

The Submission Process

Follow guidelines

It is imperative to follow each agent's submission guidelines. You can find agent's specific guidelines on their Websites, and in their online and print directory listings. Agents say the number one reason they reject a submission is due to the writer not following the guidelines. Why risk having your query discarded or dismissed because of a technicality? It is easy to follow instructions and will greatly increase the chance your query will be considered. It shows you have taken the initiative to research the agent and are conscientious of the agent's time, tastes, and needs. Many agents feel a writer who cannot follow directions during the pitching process will be a difficult client, so they will not even bother reading the pitch.

Requests for exclusivity

If an agent is interested in your project, he may ask to read your book proposal on an exclusive basis. A request for exclusivity means the agent wants to be the only one allowed to read and consider your work. He is asking that you do not share your proposal with any other agent. This can create a dilemma for an author, as it will put the submission process on hold. However, receiving an exclusivity request is a positive sign that an agent is serious about representing you.

Most writers handle requests for exclusivity by placing a limit on the time the agent has to review the material, so they are not waiting indefinitely for a response or holding up subsequent requests from other interested agents. Let the agent know that you are giving him exclusivity for a set period of time, usually two to four weeks for a book proposal. If during the exclusive time period you receive a request to review your book proposal from another agent you queried, you will have to wait until the exclusive time period is over before sending your material to the next agent. The best policy is to be honest and explain the situation.

Submitting via e-mail

Many agents prefer to receive submissions via e-mail. Here are tips to follow when submitting your pitch online:

- If possible, e-mail the agent directly (jane@theliteraryagency) instead of submitting your query to the general agency mailbox (queries@theliteraryagency). If you cannot locate the agent's direct e-mail address on the agency's Website, you may find it at Publisher's Market Place. Otherwise, call the agency and ask the receptionist for the agent's e-mail address.

- Maintain a formal presentation. Just because you are sending an e-mail does not mean it should become a casual personal note. Keep your query letter businesslike and address the agent appropriately.

- Unless otherwise specified in the agent's submission guidelines, your query letter should be contained in the body of the e-mail. Do not include attachments. Most agents will automatically delete an e-mail that contains an attachment.

- Limit your query letter to one page. Queries are meant to be only one page in length, regardless of whether you are submitting it via e-mail or snail mail. Resist the temptation to write a pitch that is longer than the accepted standard. To ensure the query adheres to the equivalent of one paper page, copy and paste it into a Word document. If it exceeds one page length, you need to shorten it.

- Do not simply send an e-mail note to an agent asking him to visit a link to your Website or blog to learn more about you and your project. That is not a query and will be ignored.

- Ensure the subject line identifies the content of the e-mail or includes wording requested by the agent. For instance, some agents state that e-mail queries should contain the subject line "query," or "nonfiction query."

- Do not use all caps or all lower case typing in your query or subject line. Use proper punctuation and grammar.

E-mail formatting

The body of an e-mail does not retain formatting. What may look professional on your computer may be incomprehensible gibberish when received by another computer. An agent may not even be reading your query on a computer - he may be viewing it on a phone with e-mail capabilities, which strips away e-mail formatting altogether. Here are tips for formatting a query letter and book proposal, when submitting via e-mail:

- Turn off the formatting in your e-mail program. Do not use bold, italics, underline, special fonts, nonstandard sizes, or colors.

- Single-space text for less than five pages of content. Double-space the text if it is more than five pages in length.

- Do not indent a paragraph.

- Use an extra space between each paragraph.

- Do not mark your e-mail as high priority.

- Do not include attachments of any kind.
- E-mail your query to yourself before sending it to the agent, to ensure the text is readable.

Submitting via standard mail

Few agents still accept query letters via snail mail. However, some experts believe that pitches submitted by mail are viewed as more important than e-mail queries and have an increased chance of receiving serious consideration. If an agent accepts submissions by standard mail and e-mail, or if the agent does not specify the method of submission, then submit your pitch using regular mail. Here are tips to follow when submitting your query by mail:

- Include an SASE (self-addressed stamped envelope). Agents receive thousands of queries each year. They cannot afford the time it takes to address envelopes to each writer or the cost of postage for each response letter that needs to be sent. If you do not include an SASE, your chances of receiving a response are slim.

- Be sure to include your complete contact information in your letter so the agent may contact you via telephone or e-mail if he chooses.

- Double-check the agency's address and the spelling of the agent's name.

- Use standardized, plain white paper and a white envelope.

What not to do when submitting your pitch

- Never send your book proposal with your query letter unless the agent's guidelines specifically request it. Some writers believe that since they are pitching the agent anyway, they might as well submit the book proposal along with their query letter and the agent will be so impressed with their writing that it will make the difference in landing representation. It will make a difference – by landing the writer's submission in the trash. Agents barely have time to read a one-page query letter; if they receive an unsolicited proposal, that submission goes at the bottom of the pile to be read last, or worse, to never be read at all.

- Do not call the agent to pitch your idea, or to tell him that you are sending the query, or to ask if the agent received your query. An agent will consider such behavior too aggressive; agents want clients who will be easy to work with, not writers who will be pushy and demanding of their time.

- Do not show up at the agent's office unannounced. Dropping off a query letter in person is probably the worst thing a writer can do to sabotage his chances of acquiring an agent. Always adhere to the agent's submission guidelines. Violating requests or exhibiting aggressive behavior turns agents off.

- Do not include gifts or props with your submission. Including an object that ties in with your book's theme may seem like a good idea, but it is not. Do not send a pen engraved with the title of your book, or a cupcake along with your pitch for a dessert cookbook. These items will not help differentiate you from the crowd; instead they make a writer appear gimmicky, amateur, and desperate.

- Do not use fancy stationary. The publishing industry is a business. Agents want to know the author understands this. Always maintain a professional businesslike presentation.

Getting to "Yes"

Agents want clients they can work with throughout the authors' careers. Here are ten things you can do to increase the chance an agent will say, "yes" to your initial pitch:

1. Ensure the first line of your pitch shows that you have done your research. Do not pitch a fitness book to an agent who

specializes in business books.

2. Let the agent know why you are approaching him specifically.

3. Tailor each pitch to the target agent. Never send a query to an agency. An author hires an individual agent, not an agency.

4. Be polite, not demanding.

5. Be willing to work with the agent on edits that will improve your chances of landing a book deal.

6. Present a tightly focused proposal. The tighter the focus of the book, the wider the potential audience. Agents do not want authors who try to be all things to everyone.

7. Be impeccably professional.

8. Show that you are determined to be a successful author, are willing to put forth the effort necessary to make it happen, and have a plan to do so.

9. Have a compelling idea for a series of books as opposed to one book.

10. Convey that you understand the publishing industry and what is expected of you.

Expert Advice: Literary Agent Jessica Faust

BookEnds, LLC
136 Long Hill Road
Gillette, NJ 07933
908-604-2652
www.bookends-inc.com
http://bookendslitagency.blogspot.com

Agency represents: current affairs, business, finance, health, women's issues, pop science, psychology, relationships, sex, parenting, pop culture, true crime, and general nonfiction.

On finding an agent: Do your research. There are many great Websites to start you off with including AAR, and Absolute Write forums. From there I think it's imperative to get as much information from individual agent Websites and blogs as possible. And then you need to follow guidelines, query, and be persistent. There is no secret to being published or finding an agent. It simply takes hard work.

On what she looks for in a book proposal: For nonfiction writers, you must have a platform. The book proposal needs to show me that the author knows the subject, including how the book differs from others on the market, and it has to be interesting to me. Oh, and of course I need to feel it's marketable.

On platform and credentials: Platform is imperative. Unless the book itself is so revolutionary that the book is the platform, I can't sell a book without a strong author platform — the media attention you get for the work you've done. This includes magazines, newspapers, radio, TV, and of course any workshops or speaking engagements you regularly do.

On trends: You should absolutely be aware of the trends. It always makes you a better businessperson to know what's going on in your business. That being said, you should never write to trends. Write what excites you.

On the process of selling the book: Once a new client signs, and we both feel the work is ready to be submitted (it's rare anything is submitted without at least some revisions first), I work on enticing editors into big offers. I keep the author updated as much as possible and encourage communication. As for time frame, there's no general anything in this business. I've sold books in 24 hours and I've had others that have taken two years. Patience is definitely a virtue.

On maintaining a good working relationship: Communicate. An agent won't and can't do a good job if you aren't communicating your concerns, wants, needs, and desires.

Chapter 6 | Crafting the Query Letter

Small to mid-size agencies receive an average of 10,000 query letters each year. With a rejection rate of 99-percent it is imperative that you carefully construct your query to receive a positive response. To achieve that, you must:

1. Know your book idea well
2. Understand where your book fits in the marketplace
3. Recognize what you have to offer as the writer

The query letter is an art form unto itself. Following are the components necessary to construct a good query letter, tips to write an effective query, and samples of successful pitches.

Components of the Query Letter

The query letter is your one-page sales pitch. It must:

- Show the agent that you are capable of quality writing
- Create excitement for your topic
- Be succinct – providing the information in as few as words as possible
- Convey that you are a professional author who understands what an agent wants

Query letters consist of four main components:

- The opening hook
- The supporting details
- The writer's qualifications
- The wrap-up

The opening hook

The first paragraph needs to do two things: establish a connection with the agent and establish the project.

Establish a connection with the agent
The first sentence of the query letter should explain why you are contacting the particular agent. Possible connections might be:

- **You read a book the agent wrote or an interview in a magazine**.
  "I recently read your interview in *Writer's Digest* magazine, where I learned you enjoy good barbecue. Because of your culinary desires I thought you might be interested in my cookbook, GOURMET SOUTHERN GRILLING..."

- **You met the agent at a conference or literary event.**
  "Thank you for speaking with me at Book Expo America last week about my business leadership book..."

- **The agent represents a similar author and genre**.
  I am a loyal Malcolm Gladwell fan. I could not put down his book *Blink*, and actually read the entire book in one day. When I learned you are his agent, I knew I wanted to query you about my own book...."

- **You discovered the agent's listing in a directory**.
  "I found your listing in Writer's Market and feel I may be a good fit for the type of writing you represent..."

- **An associate, friend, or client referred you to the agent**.
  Your author-client, Jane Meadows, referred me to you. Jane is one of my business clients and is a great supporter of my personal investment book idea...."

Establish the project
In one sentence, briefly introduce the topic or genre, the title, so the agent has an understanding of what the project is.

"HOW TO STAGE YOUR HOME TO SELL is a how-to book."

The supporting details

This section expands upon the topic. It may take one or two paragraphs. The supporting details include the theories that will be presented, the framework, who will read the book (the reader demographic), why the book is important or timely, and an overview of the content.

The writer's qualifications

The next paragraph explains why you are qualified to write the book. This section of the query letter provides an opportunity to impress the agent with your platform. You might mention the size of your blog readership, the number of speaking engagements you participate in each year, or that you host a popular weekly national radio program. If you have educational degrees, career experience, or publishing credentials, you may include those in this paragraph. Memberships in organizations, articles you have written, a list of media experience, and any contests or awards you have won should be presented.

The wrap-up

The final sentence or two are used to thank the agent for reading your query and request permission to submit additional material.

"Thank you for considering my book idea. May I send you my completed book proposal and two sample chapters?"

Query Formatting Rules

- The query letter is one page, single-spaced.
- Use Times New Roman font, 12-point.
- The title of your book is written in all caps.

For hard copy letters
- The query letter should be printed on plain letterhead or on plain paper with your name and full contact information including address, telephone, and e-mail, centered at the top of the letter.
- The first line is the date, left justified.
- Skip a line after the date, and insert the agent's name and contact information, left justified.
- Skip a line, and insert the salutation: Dear [agent's name]
- Paragraphs in the body of the letter are indented.
- Use 1-inch margins all around.

For e-mail queries
- The first line is the date
- Skip a line after the date and insert the salutation: Dear [agent name]
- Paragraphs in the body of the letter are not indented. There is a line between paragraphs.
- Your full contact information, including mailing address and telephone number is listed at the close of the letter.
- The subject line should indicate what is included in the e-mail, for instance "Query – Nonfiction Medical Title."
- Use an e-mail address that is professional and easy to remember. If possible, simply use your name, such as yourname@e-mailaddress.com.

Twelve Tips for Writing an Effective Query Letter

Nonfiction queries must focus on the writer's platform and potential market for the book. Here are 12 tips for capturing the agent's interest.

1. **Create a catchy title and introduce it early in the query letter.** Succinct, memorable titles help sell books. Show the agent you know how to write and market by crafting an appealing

title. Nonfiction titles are usually five words or less. Some books use subtitles to be more descriptive. Self-help and how-to book titles need to identify and solve the reader's problem such, as *What to Expect When You're Expecting,* and *How To Solve Your Credit Problem Now.*

2. **Show why the book is timely**
   Note any trends or media exposure that indicates a growing popularity in your subject. You do not need to find a current hot topic and craft your book idea around it, you just need to find a timely factor, such as a new study, a recent article, or a popular trend to help support your pitch.

3. **Convince the agent that you have a target market**
   Citing statistics of your potential readership shows that you understand your market niche. If you have an idea for a book about home schooling and you can quote a U.S. Department of Education report that forecasts the number of families who plan to home school their children in the next two to five years, that would be an effective statistic to include in your query and would indicate that you have a target market.

4. **Include other possible sales potentials**
   If the director of an annual festival or convention has agreed to purchase 4,000 copies of your book for next year's event, or a university plans to make it a requirement for one of its ongoing classes, then be sure to convey that sales potential in your pitch.

5. **Narrow the idea for greatest impact**
   A narrowly focused nonfiction book sells better than a broad-based one and agents are looking for narrowly defined ideas. For instance, there are hundreds of books available on the topic of home schooling. If you plan to write about home schooling, you will need to sharply focus the content of the

book. Instead of *Home Schooling for Everyone*, you might write about *Home Schooling Teenage Boys*, or *Art Projects for Home Schooling*, or *Home Schooling Assignments while Traveling in Europe*.

6. **List possible spin-offs or series ideas for the book**
   If your book idea lends itself easily to additional books, then note that in the query letter. If your book idea is *Home Schooling for Teenage Boys*, possible spin-offs might be *Home Schooling for Teenage Girls*, and *Home Schooling for First-Graders*. A series of books might include *Home Schooling for Teenage Boys: The Sciences; Home Schooling for Teenage Boys: Literature*; and *Home Schooling for Teenage Boys: History*.

7. **Differentiate your book**
   Impress the agent by conducting thorough research and presenting information to show why your book is needed. Know what other books are available and outline why your book is different from others already on the market. Perhaps other books on the topic are out-of-date, or lack information you will provide, or present a different viewpoint. Or maybe the book is needed because no other books exist on the subject.

8. **Be realistic**
   Publishers expect certain types of nonfiction books to be written by experts. If you are not a psychologist, doctor, or attorney, it is not realistic that you will be selected to write a serious book about medicine, psychiatry or legal matters. Your query must present a realistic idea that you can realistically write.

9. **Include adequate details**
   You want the agent to have a full picture of your book idea so

he can effectively consider requesting your complete proposal. A book titled *Home Schooling Teenage Boys* needs to convey more information than that it is a book about schooling teenage boys at home. Will the book provide practical solutions or be exclusively theoretical? Will it include sample assignments? Will it be written for moms, or for dads, or for both parents to read? Will it be written in a casual tone, a humorous style, or in a straight academic manner? What material and subjects will it cover? A query letter does not include every detail about the book (that is what the book proposal is for), but it should provide enough details to arouse interest and allow the agent to make an informed decision regarding requesting additional material.

10. **Drop names if you have them**
    If you have an association or connection with a celebrity, an academic, a noted author, or an authority on your subject who has agreed to write a book blurb, quote, or the foreword, it is a selling point and should be included in your query letter.

11. **List three to five things you will do to promote the book**
    Platform is key to securing a literary agent for a nonfiction book. Your promotional list should include substantial items, such as contacting your network of 50,000 followers, mentioning the book each week on your national radio show, conducting a blog and social media book tour, and distributing a series of professional produced training videos (that are tied to your book) to online video outlets.

12. **Mention self-published books only if they sold well**
    Because anyone can publish a book using today's technology, agents do not view self-published books seriously. They may believe that the book was self-published because the quality was poor, it was badly written, or it was just not good enough to garner a traditional publisher. It is best only to mention a

self-published book if it sold at least 10,000 copies, received noted media attention, or won a prestigious award.

Considerations for prescriptive nonfiction books

Practical nonfiction writers must demonstrate they can explain terms, concepts, and steps and guide the reader to a destination or goal. How-to and self-help books can take many forms, so you must be specific in your pitch about your format by explaining the general layout of the book, for instance if you will include sidebars, case studies, interviews, Q&As, anecdotes, illustrations, charts, instructions, or quizzes. If you are not an expert on the subject you plan to write about, you will also need to mention the experts that you will use as sources.

Successful Query Letter: How-To Nonfiction

Gina Cunningham
1234 Main Street
Anywhere USA, 11111
(555) 555-5555 | gina@e-mailaddress.com

August 3, 2002

Ms. Angela Miller
The Miller Agency
300 West Broadway
New York, NY 10013

Dear Ms. Miller:

   I found your listing in the "Guide to Literary Agents" and I am interested in the possibility of working together. I have an idea for a how-to nonfiction book titled MODERN TRADITIONS: INSPIRING IDEAS FOR INCORPORATING YESTERDAY'S CUSTOMS INTO

TODAY'S WEDDINGS.

This book will be the first to present cultural wedding customs with a twist: updated and reinterpreted for today's couples. I will provide inspiring suggestions on how couples can use these traditional elements in a modern way to personalize their wedding, honor their roots, and create a stylish celebration. Vibrant photographs of design elements, idea boxes, celebrity wedding references, and real couples' stories will be woven throughout the text.

As a celebrated wedding designer, coordinator, and owner of Wedding Design Studio in Los Angeles, I create and produce distinctive weddings for couples. My diverse portfolio includes both celebrity couples (actors and prominent sports figures) and everyday couples. I have been featured on several episodes of Lifetime Television's "Weddings of a Lifetime," The Today Show, and Good Morning, America. I author a bi-monthly column on theme weddings in *Inside Weddings Magazine* and speak to more than 50,000 event professionals at conferences each year. My blog, Designing Poetic Weddings, receives more than 5,000 hits per day and I have a database of 85,000 subscribers for my monthly e-newsletter. I have been featured in *Elegant Bride Magazine, Bridal Guide, Conde Nast Bride's WeddingBells, The Knot WeddingPages, InStyle Magazine, Martha Stewart Weddings*, and *The Los Angeles Times*.

I have a completed proposal and sample chapter I can send to you. Please let me know if you are interested in the book.

Thank you for your time and consideration.

Sincerely,
Gina Cunningham

Successful Query Letter: Nonfiction Anthology

Dear Mr. Sternfeld,

"Well-behaved women rarely make history," said Laurel Thatcher Ulrich.

That's because well-behaved women don't rescue men in the Wild West, discover Radium, or achieve Hollywood stardom after being fired from countless chorus-line jobs. Well-behaved women don't speed 300 miles/hour around a racetrack, trek in the Egyptian desert in full Victorian garb – and they certainly don't soar into the mysterious unknown.

Several biographies describe women who didn't behave and made history – but few anthologies provide real-life applications for readers.

What can we learn from the divas, outlaws and entrepreneurs who pursued their passions? What do they have that many of us lack? Juice, life force, energy, passion, vision, and the ability to embrace change. We have juice but life drains it. We have dreams but our mothers, partners, kids, jobs, and our own personalities can override them. We get rejected, depressed, anxious and scared... and we stop living even though we're still breathing.

SEE JANE SOAR! 200 WHO WEREN'T WELL-BEHAVED: FOLLOWING THEIR HEARTS, MAKING HISTORY:
- Presents brief, accurate profiles of historical and contemporary women from all cultures and nationalities.
- Emphasizes personality traits, achievements, and struggles. Each profile includes quotes from the woman and direct life applications for the reader.
- Highlights 10 different categories: outlaws, divas, athletes, politicians, explorers, entrepreneurs, etc. Readers can easily

access subjects that interest them.

This book offers more than a link to history. It inspires women to change and grow, to achieve their goals – whether that means earning a PhD, losing that last 10 pounds, or asking for a bank loan. Readers will see themselves in the lives of these women who courageously pursued their talents and dreams. They'll learn that Annie Oakley didn't shoot photographs and Annie Leibovitz didn't shoot targets because they followed their own hearts, minds, and souls.

SEE JANE SOAR will encourage women to accept and nurture who they truly are.

SEE JANE SOAR has the potential to morph into a calendar or daily journal for holiday or first-day-of-school gifts. A "soar" series is possible: 200 girls who didn't behave and changed history – or 200 Canadians, seniors, athletes, teachers, people with disabilities, people with diseases, and so on.

My degrees in Education and Psychology give me a solid background with which to research and write this book. I lived and taught in Africa for three years and traveled worldwide – I know how exciting it is to soar!

And I write. My publications include articles for *Woman's Day, Flare, Reader's Digest, Glow, alive, Esteem, Good Times, Today's Health and Wellness,* and *Cahoots.*

Let me know if you'd like to review a full book proposal.

Yours truly,
Laurie Pawlik-Kienlen

Do's and Don'ts of Query Letter Writing

Below is a checklist compiled from professional agents' requests.

- Do get to the point. Agents are busy people. They only have a limited amount of time to consider your project. Do not ramble on about non-consequential things. If you cannot write a tight, pertinent pitch, how will you write a succinct book?

- Do follow the correct format and keep the letter to only one page. The format of your letter demonstrates you are a professional author who understands what is required. A pitch that is longer than one page (or two at the very most) stands a good chance of never being read.

- Do not compare your work to known authors. Positioning your book alongside other published works in style, subject, or readership is acceptable but do not compare the quality of your writing to established authors. Stating "I am the next Seth Godin" will make you appear conceited, not confident. Your writing will speak for itself. There is already one Seth Godin, and there is only one you, so resist comparing yourself and your writing to other authors.

- Do mention that you have queried multiple agents. It is professional and demonstrates you understand how the business works.

- Do not discuss money, contracts or film deals. Doing so makes you appear amateurish and aggressive. Your job is to capture the agent's interest for your work. Payment, royalties, subsidiary rights, and other contract details are negotiated once a publisher makes an offer to purchase your book.

LAURA CROSS: Get Published

- Do not send your letter certified mail. Doing so may annoy the agent.

- Do not introduce yourself by starting the letter with "My name is..." Your name is included in your contact information and with your signature.

- Do not use the term "novel" for a nonfiction book. Novels are exclusively fiction.

- Do not state that you are writing a query or seeking representation. If an agent is reading your letter he knows it is a query and that you are seeking representation.

- Do include information about a previously published book if it sold at least 10,000 copies. Agents say it is easier to place a debut book than it is a book by an author who has a mixed sales track-record. A previously published book is only an advantage if it sold very well. If it did, then mention it, but keep the focus of the query on your new project.

- Do not mention that your family and friends love your book idea. The agent does not care what non-writers think about your book. Your work should speak for itself.

- Do not submit a query letter if you have not finished writing the book proposal. An agent cannot evaluate a project if the proposal is not complete and available to review. An agent wants to be able to shop the book idea to a publisher immediately and will not wait for you to finish the required material.

- Do not demand that the agent read your work or threaten to take it elsewhere. Threats and demands immediately identify you as an amateur and someone who will be difficult to work with. Stating in a query letter that if the agent does not take you on as a client that she will be missing out on the next bestseller does not encourage an agent to consider you as a client, instead it demonstrates how unprofessional the author is and leads to the agent dismissing the pitch completely.

- Do not submit a query that does not fit the agent's requirements for genre. Do not waste your time, or the agent's, attempting to convince her to represent your business book if she does not represent that genre simply because you think it is a great book. It may be, but agents specialize in specific titles and have cultivated resources and expertise in selling those particular titles – they do not suddenly change their

- Do not pitch multiple submissions to an agent. Simultaneous submissions, querying more than one agent at the same time, are acceptable, but multiple submissions, pitching more than one project to the same agent at the same time, is considered unprofessional.

How I Acquired My Agent: Jan Dunlap

Website: **www.jandunlap.com**

Books: *Purpose, Passion and God: Awakening to the Deepest Meaning of Life* (Twenty-third Publications, 2006)
Genre: theology and spirituality.

I have had three books published without an agent and for my newest project, I wanted to pitch into a national market and realized I needed an agent for those contacts.

I approached about ten agents before finding the right one. None of the rejection letters offered any advice or direction for improvement so I kept polishing my query letter to make it irresistible. I looked at a list of agents who would be at a local writing conference and chose one of them to pitch, based on her bio. Then I studied the company's Website and realized I needed to pitch her partner instead, so I did that via e-mail. He called me within hours of receiving my e-mail query and we had a long phone discussion about our spiritual perspectives and professional expectations. I was sure it was 'meant to be.'

Chapter 7 | Creating the Book Proposal

A book proposal is a marketing tool used to present and sell your nonfiction book idea to a publisher before you write the book. It is the only means for selling a nonfiction book to a commercial publisher.

Writing a book proposal benefits you in several ways: it saves you time and effort, and allows you to receive partial payment prior to writing the full manuscript.

The Purpose of a Book Proposal

Many nonfiction authors mistakenly believe that if they write a full manuscript they can send it off to an agent to be sold to a publisher. But agents and editors do not review nonfiction manuscripts, unless they are narrative nonfiction such as memoir or history.

A book proposal is required to sell a nonfiction book. A nonfiction manuscript does not answer the editorial review committee's questions about marketing, competition, production, or the author's platform. A publisher will invest tens of thousands of dollars to develop a book and requires a complete view of the project (which the book proposal provides) prior to making a decision.

What the book proposal does:
- Introduces the topic of your book
- Explains why you are qualified to write the book
- Includes sample chapters showcasing the content and your writing ability
- Provides a market analysis of competitive books

- Contains logistical information about the book, such as the length, delivery, and format (sidebars, expert interviews, photos, and charts)
- Analyzes the market for the book (who will buy your book)
- Presents your platform and marketing and promotional ideas to help sell the book

Editors and agents are overwhelmed by submissions and must choose the most well written proposals. Many book proposal submissions are poorly written or do not answer the fundamental questions necessary for an editor or agent to make an informed decision. By writing a compelling book proposal you will have the edge over your competition and be better positioned to have your book published.

The Components Of A Book Proposal

The book proposal varies in length from 10 to 40 pages, plus the pages of the sample chapter(s), based on the scope of your specific project. It consists of the following sections:

- The title page
- The proposal table of contents
- The overview
- The market
- Competitive analysis
- The promotional plan
- About the author and platform
- The chapter outline
- Sample chapters
- Supplemental material

The overview

The overview section summarizes what your book is about. It needs to concisely convey what you intend to write and generate interest in the project.

The book proposal should begin with a strong hook. The opening paragraph must evoke excitement in the reader. Effective leads include an anecdote or case study, an interesting fact or statistic, an appropriate quotation that captures the style and tone of your subject, or a compelling question that provokes thought and consideration.

For the remaining overview section, you need to:
- Identify the subject and scope of the book
- Present why the book is important or needed
- Include a brief overview of the production details

List the benefits and the features of your book. Then state why your book is unique or timely. Close the overview section with an outline of the book's:
- Special features - such as sidebars, images, charts, quizzes, case studies, checklists or illustrations
- Structure - an explanation of the parts, chapters, and sections of the book
- Estimated word count or page count
- Estimated delivery

The market
The market for your book refers to the audience. Agents and publishers want to know there is a large targeted group of readers who will purchase the book when it is released. In this section, you need to:

- Identify the people who will buy your book
- Provide supporting evidence that the market is viable
- Demonstrate the potential for spin-offs or a series of books
- Explain any special sales avenues

Who is the market
It is important to identify a large, targeted, specific group of potential readers who want or need what you plan to write about. Include demographic details such as gender, age range, education, income, social class, and lifestyle in your description (for instance, "Retired African-American women who have survived breast cancer" or "Teenage girls between the ages of 12 and 14 who struggle with math.") It may be tempting to state that the market for your book is "everyone" or "all women", but in reality very few books attain that level of mass appeal.

Books targeted to a specific group of people sell far more copies than non-targeted books, so show an agent and publisher that there is a specific target market for your book. Instead of saying your potential readers are "Guys who like to go hiking with their dogs", present a more detailed description, such as "Adventurous males over 40 who own dogs and enjoy backpacking throughout the western United States."

How large is the market
If the potential market for your book is only 5,000, it will be challenging to find an agent and a traditional publisher for your book. It is essential that your book's market not only be specific and targeted, but also large enough to warrant publication.

- Mention the popularity of similar books
- Include statistics on the topic to support your claims (for example, "In 2011, the oldest of the baby boomer generation, those born in 1946, will turn 65 years old. Fifty-one percent of them are women, and an estimated 4.6 million of those women are African-American…")
- Cite studies and reports
- Use magazine and newspaper articles that indicate an increased trend toward your subject (for instance, "According

to an article in *The New York Times* in January 2009, green construction is on the rise...")
- Note the number of members belonging to associations, trade groups and organizations who would be interested in your topic.

There are many resources available to help you determine how many potential readers there are for your subject matter:
- Browse the bestseller lists for similar titles
- Use Internet search-engines to find articles and interesting facts
- For statistical information, peruse the *American Statistical Index* or *Statistical Source*, available at your local library
- For statistics on the number of books sold annually in a specific genre, review *The Bowker Annual Library and Book Trade Almanac*
- Read the *Encyclopedia of Associations* to find membership information on just about any type of organization. Available at most public libraries, this book provides an extensive list of thousands of associations on almost any topic
- *Directories In Print* provides a comprehensive, annotated listing of more than 10,000 business and industrial directories and guides published in the United States

Series or spin-off potential
Spin-off or series potential is not mandatory to sell your book idea, but an agent or publisher is more interested in projects that begat more product. Books with spin-off or series potential are considered more valuable than stand-alone books. *The Chicken Soup for the Soul* series has spawned more than 100 books including *Chicken Soup for the Soul: Power Moms*; *Chicken Soup for the Military Wife's Soul*; and *Chicken Soup for the Soul: What I Learned From My Dog*, as well as a substantial amount of licensed products from greeting cards to calendars. Think of ways your book could become a series or generate spin-offs.

Special sales avenues
Publishers will distribute your book through the normal channels – large retail bookstore chains and online outlets, such as Amazon.com and Barnes and Noble. These are considered primary sales avenues. If you can present opportunities for secondary sales avenues – such as via independent local bookstores, specialty retail stores, institution sales, libraries, or educational courses - you increase your chances of landing a book deal.

If you're writing a book about organic food, you could mention the number of small bookstores throughout the country that specialize in cookbooks, retail chains that sell culinary related products (such as William-Sonoma and Sur La Table), health-food stores, resorts and retreats that focus on fitness and nutrition, universities and community colleges that teach organic cooking classes, or large Farmer's Markets across the country. Be creative and think outside the box for any potential sales avenue that would be a good fit for your book's topic. Your own Website may also be an avenue for selling the book, so be sure to mention it.

Competitive analysis
The purpose of the competitive analysis section is to convince an agent and publisher that there is room on the bookstore shelf for your book. A competitive analysis consists of reviewing and comparing your book idea to six to twelve other similar books on the market and demonstrating why your book will be better or different from the competitive titles. The list of books in the competitive analysis section also informs the agent and publisher where you envision your book in the marketplace.

Amazon.com is an excellent source for identifying similar books. Go to **www.amazon.com** and enter a keyword search for your book idea. Their search-engine will produce a list of current books on your topic that you can research further. Review the table of contents (using the "Search inside this book" tool) and note the topics addressed in the book. Once you have found the six to twelve most appropriate books for comparison you will need to either purchase the books or obtain them from your local library. For each book, read a few chapters and identify the approach, point of view, structure, scope and style. Also check the bibliography and note if the sources the author used differ from your list (which may indicate a difference in perspective and material covered.)

To create the comparative competitive analysis:

1. Begin with a lead that restates the need for your book and why it differs from others on the market.

2. Provide an analysis and comparison of each book that includes:
    *   Bibliographical information for the competitive title
    *   A statement of the competitive book's intentions
    *   An assessment of how that book's information is presented and how effective the book delivers on its promise
    *   A few sentences explaining what differentiates your book's goals from the competitive book's aims
    *   Key points of what you book will offer that is more useful or interesting than the other book (remember, you want to critique the book, but do not directly insult the writer or the book)

3. Conclude the section by summarizing why your book is better than the other titles.

The promotional plan

The promotional plan details what you will do to help sell the book. Agents and publishers want to know you are willing and capable of marketing the book by evaluating your plan, your platform, and your connections. Your promotional plan may also provide the publishing house's marketing department with additional ideas for how to best promote your book.

The promotional plan should be detailed, specific, and realistic. For instance:

- "I have six speaking engagements at large conferences scheduled for next year, where I will deliver keynote addresses to more than 50,000 attendees."
- "I will produce a book trailer which will appear on my Website that receives over 15,000 unique visitors each day and also publish it on YouTube."
- "I will highlight the book on my weekly nationally syndicated radio show with more than 80,000 listeners."
- "I will pre-sell the title though my monthly newsletter of more than 60,000 subscribers."
- "I will tweet excerpts from the book via Twitter where I have 96,000 followers."

Do not present vague statements, such as "I will promote the book on *Oprah*". Include concrete information: "I have received an invitation to appear on *Oprah,* once the book has been published."

About the author

The 'about the author' section of the proposal presents your biographical information and expands upon your promotional ability. The purpose of this section is to:

- Establish your credibility as the best person to write the book
- Demonstrate that your name or persona will help sell the book
- Give the agent and publisher a sense of who you are as a person

The about the author section may be written in either first or third person perspective. All the information you present should confirm your ability to write and sell the book. This section addresses the following areas:

Platform

A strong platform is essential to acquiring a book deal. This section may be the most important and most influential of the entire proposal. Present detailed, specific information to show that you have a strong, established platform that continues to grow.

Mention your Website, blogs, television and radio exposure, print interviews, published articles, number of Facebook fans, Twitter followers, and LinkedIn connections, note how many subscribers you have for your newsletter or e-mail campaigns, highlight major speaking engagements, and if you have previously published a successful book include the sales figures.

Credentials

You want to show the agent and publisher that you are a recognized expert on the topic you plan to write about. You can demonstrate this by highlighting your:

- Subject credentials ("I am the columnist for *Financial Times*, a respected financial journal read by investors and CEOs.")
- Career credentials ("I have been the Vice-President of Wealth Management Services for more than ten years, where I manage investments for Fortune 500 executives.")
- Educational background ("I earned my PhD in Finance from Harvard.")
- Relevant awards or professional memberships ("I have been honored with the prestigious Golden Wealth Mentor award and serve as Director for the Professional League of Finance."

The chapter outline

The purpose of this section is to present a preview of the entire book. An agent wants to know that you will cover all the intended information, deliver the book's promise within the content, and package it in a form that is accessible to readers. The chapter outline presents the book's table of contents followed by a summary of each chapter.

Sample chapters

Sample chapters are excerpts from your book that highlight your writing ability, and the style, tone, and depth of the manuscript. Each agent has different criteria for the number of sample chapters or pages he or she may request. Some agents may only ask for one chapter, others may want to see three chapters, and still others may request a specific number of pages. Plan to write the first two chapters, or at least the first thirty pages of your book, for possible submission.

Supplemental material

The supplemental material section, also referred to as the appendix, is optional. However, most agents advise including it when possible. This section contains additional items about you and your subject. Items you may consider submitting include:

- Published writing samples – may include magazine, newspaper, or online articles you have written related to your topic
- Material about you – profiles and articles that have been written about you
- Promotional material - such as business brochures, booklets, and conference publications
- A color or black and white headshot – the headshot is a common inclusion in a book proposal and should be a professional 8"x10" photograph, similar to an author's photo on a book. If you have a quality photograph of yourself

participating in an activity that relates to the book, such as cooking, or surfing, or painting, you may choose to include it

- Published material about your book's subject - photocopies of recent articles or features about the topic and its popularity
- Summary of radio interviews and television appearances (if available, consider including a short, professionally produced clip on DVD)
- A selection from your portfolio – only if your portfolio is relevant and directly relates to your topic (for instance, if your book is about arranging flowers you could include a selection of your best floral designs)
- A few sample images, charts, diagrams or illustrations that you plan to insert in the book

Formatting and Packaging Your Book Proposal

The presentation of your book proposal is as important as the content. Print the proposal on white 24 lb. paper with black ink and one-inch margins. Use a standard, easy to read font, such as Calibri, Times New Roman or Arial, 12-point. All text is double-spaced, except your contact information, which is listed on the title page. Paragraphs are indented.

The title page

The title page is the first page of your proposal. Centered, one-third of the way down from the top of the page, is the title and author listing:

A Proposal for
Title of your book (printed in either all capital letters or italicized)
Subtitle or tagline of the book
by (your name)

In the lower left or right corner of the page, your contact information is listed:

- Your mailing address
- Your telephone number
- Your e-mail address

The proposal's table of contents
The first page after the title page is the proposal's table of contents. List each part of the proposal, flush left with the corresponding page number listed flush right.

The body of the proposal
Each page should be numbered consecutively. The page number is placed in the upper right corner. In the upper left corner of the page include a header listing your last name and the title of the book (the title is printed in either all capital letters or italicized) divided by a slash: Author's last name / BOOK TITLE.

Supplemental material
All newspaper and magazine clips and additional material, such as brochures and booklets, should be presented on 8 ½ x 11 paper. If necessary, photocopy the documents to conform to the correct size.

Packaging the proposal
Book proposals are usually presented in a sturdy double-pocket folder. Do not staple the pages together. Place the complete proposal and sample chapters in one pocket and the supplemental material in the other pocket.

(See Appendix II for a sample of a successful book proposal)

The Top Ten Reasons Book Proposals Are Rejected

1. **The proposal does not contain a strong argument for why the topic is relevant, timely and necessary.**
   How to fix the problem: cite forecasts, statistics, and recent media attention surrounding the subject.

2. **There is nothing to differentiate this book from similar books on the topic.**
   How to fix the problem: present a well-developed slant on the topic and clearly show how your book is different and why it is better than similar titles.

3. **The author's platform is not developed enough to indicate viable sales**.
   How to fix the problem: establish and grow your platform with increased media exposure, ongoing publicity, and an extensive network of connections.

4. **The writing in the sample chapters is weak or not compelling or the author's writing style is overly academic.**
   How to fix the problem: use active voice and include stories in your writing to engage the reader, enroll in writing workshops to become a better writer, or hire an editor or ghostwriter to polish the chapters.

5. **The author did not identify a specific, target market.**
   How to fix the problem: carefully define your readers.

6. **The market is too small**.
   How to fix the problem: include statistics and specialty marketing strategy suggestions.

7. **The author lacks credentials.**
   How to fix the problem: if you are not an expert on the topic, consider working with a co-author or obtaining the required credentials.

8. **The book will cost too much to produce.**
   How to fix the problem: reduce the number of suggested images and lower the estimated page count.

9. **The author presented an article, not a book.**
   How to fix the problem: widen your topic so it will qualify as a full manuscript and expand your chapter summary.

10. **The author outlined an unrealistic marketing plan.**
    How to fix the problem: create a practical promotional plan with strong, specific strategies.

How I Acquired My Agent: Lisa Lawmaster Hess

Website: **www.L2Hess.com**
Blog: **www.L2Hess.blogspot.com**

Books: *Acting Assertively* and *Diverse Divorce*
Genre: Self-help
Agent: Diana Flegal, Hartline Literary Agency

I met my agent Diana at the Susquehanna Valley Writers' Conference. I had made an appointment with her. We just clicked. She was so friendly and upbeat, she offered all sorts of positive feedback. She had as much enthusiasm for my project as I did, so I knew she would represent it well.

The best advice I can five is to be honest about what you can and cannot do, but also be willing to take risks. Do your part - keep

LAURA CROSS: Get Published 105

writing, build that platform, keep informed and keep reading in your genre. Respect your agent as a person and as a professional, and remember that although your work is your baby, your agent is representing many other people's babies, too, so your's is not an only child. Do not allow bad feelings to fester - if you have frustrations, express them respectfully. Remember, too, that your agent wants to help you build a career, so keep writing.

SECTION III:

HIRING A LITERARY AGENT

Chapter 8 | Waiting For A Response

The amount of time you will need to wait for a response after submitting your pitch will differ for each agent. During this time, you may receive rejection letters, continue pitching to other agents, follow up with agents who fail to respond, and receive requests to submit additional material.

Use Your Time Wisely

While waiting for a response to your query letter, book proposal submission you want to continue to prepare for your career as an author. You can use this waiting period to:

1. **Begin formulating your next book idea**
   Every author and literary agent interviewed for this book agreed that the number one thing every writer needs to do while waiting for a response is to outline his or her next book idea.

2. **Continue to build your platform**
   Increase your social networking activities, expand your blogging to include guest posts on other writers' sites, author articles, and make yourself available as a resource for reporters, journalists, and radio show hosts as a way to garner additional media exposure.

3. **Prepare your next set of query letters**
   When you have a stack of query letters prepared and waiting to be sent, any time you receive a rejection letter from one agent you will not have to waste time dwelling on the disappointment because you are ready to contact the next one – and increase your chances of becoming published.

4. **Improve your writing skills**

   The more you write, the better writer you become. The better writer you are, the more valuable, viable, and marketable your material will be. Devote more time to writing each day. There are many excellent books on the craft of writing that can help you, such as *The Elements of Story: Field Notes on Nonfiction Writing* by Francis Flaherty. Online and onsite writing classes, workshops, seminars, conferences, and groups can also improve your skills.

Expert Advice: Literary Agent Rachelle Gardner

WordServe Literary Group
Website: **www.WordServeLiterary.com**
Blog: **http://cba-ramblings.blogspot.com**
Twitter: @RachelleGardner
E-mail: rachelle@wordserveliterary.com

On the types of authors and genres she is looking for: I'm looking for books that don't contradict a Christian worldview. In nonfiction, I'm looking at Christian market and general market projects: Home Life, Marriage, Parenting, Family, Current Affairs, Crafts, Health & Diet, How-to, Humor, Memoirs, Money, Narrative Nonfiction, Popular Culture, Psychology, Science, Self-Help, and Women's Issues.

On what constitutes a good query letter: A good query pitches the book in a way that makes me want to read it, and also includes a small amount of relevant information about the author. The point of a query isn't to tell the whole story, but to make someone want to read the story.

On the importance of an author's platform: For nonfiction, the author platform is a very important consideration. You need to show that you have a built-in audience of potential book buyers, and that you have credibility in your topic. How to build a platform depends on what you're writing about; but anyone can begin to build a following through a blog and online social networking.

On being aware of publishing trends: Authors should write whatever they want, but base their publishing expectations on realistic evaluation of the market.

On crafting a nonfiction book proposal: The "competitive books" section is one of the most important parts. It's crucial to show the publisher that you know what else has already been written that's similar. It's also crucial to make your "author marketing" section as impressive as possible, without including any "wishes" or things you're willing to do. (Don't say, "Author is willing to promote, do book signings, radio interviews.") Only include things you will do and things you have the ability to make happen.

On maintaining a good agent/author working relationship: It sounds cliché but as with all relationships, communication is key. When you are confused about something, or disagree with something, it's crucial to discuss it with your agent. If you don't, misunderstandings can fester.

When to Follow Up

Most agents' submission guidelines, available on their Websites and in print listings, outline the agent's average response time for queries, books proposals, and manuscripts. This should give you a good idea of when to expect to hear from a particular agent. The average response time for:

- Query letters is two to four weeks
- Book proposals is four to six weeks

If you have not received a response from an agent within two to three weeks past the date of his or her listed response time, you should follow up with the agent. For follow-ups to book proposals, it is perfectly acceptable to call the agent and inquire if he or she has had time to review the material. For follow-ups to queries, you may send a brief note along with a copy of the original query letter.

Dear [Mr. Agent]:

I am following up on a query that I submitted to you eight weeks ago for my nonfiction book idea, MODERN TRADITIONS. As I have not received a response, I was not sure if my original letter landed on your desk or was lost somewhere in cyberspace. I am resubmitting my query pasted below.

Thank you for your time and consideration. I hope to hear from you soon.

Sincerely,
[Author's name and contact information]

[Original query letter]

Learning From Rejection

Rejection is an uncomfortable part of the submission process. Like all published authors, you will most likely receive many rejection letters. It is important, for your own peace of mind and for your professional success as an author, to maintain a positive attitude and persevere until you acquire an agent and land a book deal. Authors Jack Canfield and Mark Victor received 144 rejections before obtaining an agent and a publishing deal, and their book,

Chicken Soup for the Soul, went on to become a New York Times bestseller.

Sometimes, rejection can be a gift. If the agent gives you notes, her advice can help you make constructive revisions and lead to an improved proposal. Most agents are too busy to have the time to write editorial notes. If you are lucky enough to receive feedback from an agent, be sure to send her a thank-you by e-mail or postcard, and inquire if you may resubmit the work once you have made the suggested changes. Do not be discouraged if the agent will not accept the revised submission, simply move on and pitch the next agent on your list.

The more common type of rejection is a form rejection letter – a standard form the agent sends out when he or she chooses not to represent an author. Even though a form rejection letter does not provide specific advice to help guide your rewrite, it does provide a definite response, which releases you from waiting limbo and allows you to continue pitching other agents – and move closer to your goal of becoming a published author.

Tips For Submitting Additional Requested Material

When an agent requests additional material, such as your book proposal, it is important to remain as professional and responsive as when you sent the initial query.

1. **Send the requested material immediately.**
   Agents report they are perplexed when authors send material weeks or even months after it has been requested. If an agent is intrigued enough by your query to want to learn more about your nonfiction project, send it immediately. Do not wait. If you do you risk the agent losing interest, forgetting about you

and your book, or deciding that you are unprofessional and not worth representing.

2. **Send the requested material via priority delivery service.**
   The purpose of using a priority delivery service is to ensure the material arrives in a timely manner to the right destination (on the agent's desk and not in the assistant's 'slush pile'.)

3. **Include a copy of the agent's request.**
   Often an intern or assistant will open the package. Inserting a copy of the agent's request for your material, along with a copy of the original query letter or a brief cover letter, indicates the material was solicited and ensures it will be delivered directly to the agent for review.

4. **Send only what is requested.**
   Be sure to send exactly what the agent has requested. Remember, following an agent's instructions demonstrates that you are a professional author who is easy to work with.

5. **Consider making requested revisions**.
   Sometimes after reviewing the additional requested material, an agent will respond with a request asking you to make specific changes to your proposal and then to resubmit it. You will need to consider whether you wish to make the changes, if the revisions will benefit the material or project, and if you wish to continue to pursue possible representation from the agent. When an agent takes the time to comment on your material, it is usually because he feels there is good potential for selling the book and he is seriously considering representing you. If you feel comfortable with the agent's requests then it may be in your best interest to make the revisions and resubmit the material for a second consideration.

Expert Advice: Literary Agent Joanna Stampfel-Volpe

Nancy Coffey Literary & Media Representation
240 West 35th Street, Suite 500
New York, NY 10001

Joanna represents: narrative nonfiction (environmental, foodie, and pop culture).

On how to find an agent: Research. I can't tell you how many writers I reject because they've queried me with something I'm not even looking for.

On what makes query letter good: It has to follow industry standards: single page, size twelve font, one inch margins, contact info included, genre and word count. It might seem obvious, but many authors don't follow these basic guidelines. After that, what constitutes a good query letter to me is one that tells me about the book.

On being aware of trends: Authors should always be aware of publishing trends because they should be reading. A lot. Especially in the genre they write in. But that doesn't mean they should write for the trends. You should always write what you're passionate about. Always.

On "finding" authors: I do find authors. I read blogs, magazines and anthologies all the time. I recently contacted a journalist I've been following.

On how an author can learn from rejection: Even if the author receives a number of form rejections with no personal advice given, it's just another step in the process. There is rejection throughout this entire industry. Writers get rejected from agents. Agents get rejections from editors. Editors can get rejections on a project from their peers, boss or sales. Sales can get rejections from book buyers. And then the reviews come out - the reading public can be harsh! From every rejection along the way, it will hopefully make the author a little bit stronger and even more determined. Meanwhile, a writer should always be in the process of honing their craft. No matter how many books you have published, there is always more to learn.

On what happens once a client is signed: The time frame varies drastically. I take a very active editorial role as long as the client is comfortable with that, so I will go back and forth with revisions, I get them second readers in-house, and I line edit when necessary. Once a project is ready for submission, I write up my submission list.

For every project it's different. I've done careful research and I choose editors who I truly think would be a good fit for the project and the author. It takes me a few days or more to write up my pitch letter, but when I first go out with it, it's over the phone. I like to show the editors how excited I am about the project and I like to gauge their initial reactions. Once I know which editors are reading the work, I e-mail the author the list of which houses are considering their work. Then, we wait. And wait. And sometimes wait some more.

During that time I'm actively following up with the editors and I'll even start working on the author's next project if there is something already to work on. As responses come back, I keep the author updated in a way that they feel comfortable. Some authors really want to know the minute a rejection comes in. Some want to wait until a few responses come in before I let them know. Either way, I'm always in communication with my clients about the process.

Tips for maintaining a good working relationship: Be patient. Agents have multiple clients and have to give attention to each one of them, and more importantly, agents have a job to do. I don't know of a single agent who just idles around all day. We're in meetings, having lunch with editors, negotiating contracts, submitting projects, editing manuscripts, reading submissions, attending conferences, reading queries and handling day-to-day issues/office work.

Your agent wouldn't have signed you if they didn't believe in your writing, even if that first project isn't the one to sell - we simply just don't have time to take on things we're not 110% enthusiastic about. Your agent is one of your biggest champions in the industry, and he/she has your best interest in mind always (don't forget—your best interest is his/her best interest!). Don't expect daily, weekly or even monthly correspondence. I know you're anxious to get published, and if I'm your agent, I'm anxious for you to get published too. But I also want to make sure that we start or continue your career in the strongest way possible.

Chapter 9 | Evaluating an Agent's Offer

When an agent is excited to represent you, he or she will often telephone you to make an offer or send you a personal note. Every writer knows that finding an agent can be a difficult process. Many authors simply sign a contract with the first agent who offers representation. Selecting an agent is a serious business decision and should be carefully considered. You want to ensure the agent is the best one for your book and the right match for your writing career.

Questions to Ask the Agent You May Hire

Many of your potential questions about your prospective agent (such as the size of the agency, how many books she's sold in the past year, her specialties, the different publishers she has worked with, and how long she has been in business) will already be answered before you receive an offer of representation (you would have garnered this information from the research you conducted prior to approaching her.) After you have received an offer of representation, other important questions will arise. The responses you receive from the agent will help you evaluate if you should sign with her.

Schedule an appointment via telephone or in person to discuss your questions. The discussion should be a balanced exchange of information, you do not want to appear to be 'grilling' or 'interrogating' your prospective agent by reading from a long list of prepared questions. Let the exchange unfold naturally and choose to ask only a handful of the most important questions (based on your individual needs.) Here is a list of questions you may wish to ask:

1. **Are you a member of the Association of Author's Representatives?**
There are many excellent agents who are not members of the AAR but lack of sales and charging fees are two reasons an agent may be denied membership. If the agent is not a member, ask him why he is not and if he still adheres to their ethical guidelines.

2. **How do you feel about my book and its potential?**
The response you receive will help you gage her enthusiasm for the project. You need an agent who will champion your book and not give up after receiving a few rejections.

3. **Do you feel the proposal needs edits before you begin pitching the book to publishers?**
Her response will give you an idea of the scope of edits she is expecting and how long it will take to make the changes before she actually begins selling the project. It can also help you decide if you agree with her comments and are willing to make the requested revisions.

4. **How do you plan to market my book?**
The agent should be able to provide a clear strategy to sell your book. Will she pitch to several publishers at once or only one at a time? How many editors will she approach and what publishing houses will she submit to? If she cannot illustrate her plan, then she may be a disorganized and ineffective salesperson.

5. **How often should I contact you?**
It's best to have an understanding of expectations regarding communication before entering an agreement with the agent. If your hope is to be able to contact her once a week and she implies that anything more than once per month is

inappropriate, then she is probably not the right agent for you.

6. **How often should I expect to receive updates?**
   It is important to determine if you are a match regarding correspondence. Are you comfortable receiving an e-mail update once every two months or do you prefer contact by telephone at least twice per month?

7. **Will you forward copies of rejection letters to me?**
   Obtaining copies of rejection letters from publishers is one of the few tools you can use to determine how productive your agent is in pitching your book. Some agents do not send rejection letters to their clients, but instead provide a monthly or quarterly summary of their marketing efforts. If you have a specific preference, be sure you select an agent who will deliver what you need.

8. **How many authors do you currently represent?**
   If she represents a small number of clients she will likely have plenty of time to focus on you and your book – but do ask why she has so few clients. If the number of clients she represents is large (more than 50), ask her how she manages so many authors. Does she have assistants and sub-agents? Find out how she plans to provide the attention necessary for your book to succeed.

9. **How many of your current clients are published?**
   The percentage of authors for whom she has actually landed a book deal can provide insight into her sales ability.

10. **On average how many [insert genre] books do you sell a year?**
    If your prospective agent represents a variety of nonfiction genres but she has only sold business books and you write cookbooks, it may indicate that -- while she may be

enthusiastic about cooking and want to represent you -- she may lack the experience and connections to garner publishing deals for your genre. In such a case, if you decide to proceed with her as your agent, ensure she has a strong marketing strategy in place for your book - not simply an enthusiastic attitude.

11. **What commissions do you charge?**
The standard industry commission is 15 percent. You should not be charged a higher rate. If the agent offers a "reduced commission" plus a small "representation fee" – run fast in the other direction because such an "offer" is a scam.

12. **Am I responsible for any other expenses?**
Some legitimate agents may charge a nominal fee for photocopies, priority mailing costs, and faxing services. If an agent charges any other type of fee it is an indication that the agent is not reputable.

13. **What subsidiary rights have you sold for your clients and how is that handled?**
You want an agent who is competent in selling different types of subsidiary rights – book clubs, film rights, foreign rights, audio, serial rights. If your agent lacks this skill you risk losing potential profits and exposure you would otherwise acquire with the sale of subsidiary rights. Some agencies have in-house departments that exclusively handle subsidiary rights. Some agents sub-contract other agents to handle the sales of these rights. For instance, your agent may work with a literary agent in Hollywood to handle selling film and television rights because the Hollywood agent has better connections in the entertainment industry. It is always to the author's benefit to have subsidiary rights retained by the agent. If your prospective agent informs you that she usually allows the publisher to retain the rights, you need to consider how such a

policy will impact your long-term career.

14. **What is your procedure and timeframe for payment of authors' royalties and advances received from the publisher?**
All payments due to you from your publisher will be paid to your agent. Your agent deducts his or her commission and any additional agreed upon expenses from the publisher's check and then issues you the remaining balance. An ethical agent who follows standard business practices should have a non-interest bearing 'holding' account for client monies that is entirely separate from the agency bank account. You want to deal with an efficient and organized agent who will issue your payment to you in a timely manner. Her response to this question should indicate that she has good business practices and a well-managed system in place for sending authors' payments.

15. **Do you issue an IRS 1099 form at the end of the year?**
The Internal Revenue Service requires businesses to provide an annual 1099 form for each individual (who is not an employee) to whom the company has paid a certain amount of money. Your prospective agent should be set up to easily produce these forms each year. If she is not, it is an indication that her accounting practices are lax.

16. **If you do not sell my book within a specific period of time, what happens?**
Will the agent drop you as a client, allow you the option to find another agent, or continue to work with you to create another project to pitch?

17. **How involved are you with guiding your clients' careers?**
Your prospective agent's response will indicate her level of commitment to an author's career.

18. **What happens when a publisher makes an offer, do you handle all the negotiations or do you consult with the author regarding the particulars?**
    Some authors prefer to be involved in every detail, while others are comfortable allowing their agents to control all the terms. Choose an agent whose method is right for you.

19. **What happens if you go out of business, leave the agency, or pass away?**
    If it is a large agency, will another agent take over your representation, or will you have the option to hire an agent elsewhere? If the agent moves to another firm, will the agent take you with her to the new agency? If the agency closes, what will happen to your royalty statements and subsequent payments? You want to obtain a written agreement that outlines every possible form of exit.

20. **Do you have an agent-author contract?**
    Some agents do not work with written agreements. It is unwise to hire an agent without a written contract. You are entering into a legal business partnership. A contract protects both parties by outlining goals, limits, and responsibilities.

Avoiding Scams and Assuring Credibility

Unfortunately, unscrupulous people exist in any industry, and the literary world is no exception. Anyone can call himself a literary agent, buy business cards, accept writer submissions, and take advantage of unsuspecting authors. When you have an understanding of how legitimate literary agents operate you will be more able to protect yourself from predators. It pays to be knowledgeable and stay aware.

Here is a list of "agent" practices to avoid:

- **Inappropriate fees**
  Legitimate literary agents do not charge fees to read writers' proposals. Nor do they charge critiquing fees, retainers, or upfront office administrative or marketing fees.

- **Referrals to editing or book doctoring services**
  A fake literary agent may tell you she likes your book idea but that it just needs some work and for a fee she can edit it for you or refer you to a book doctor. In reality, this is a scam to collect your money without improving the work. If a "so-called" agent offers this service, move on to another agent.

- **No sales record**
  Professional literary agents will discuss their recent sales with a prospective client. They should be able to tell you how many books they've sold, what types of books they sold, and to whom they were sold.

- **Refusing to answer questions**
  A good agent will respectfully answer your inquiries and allow you to make the final decision concerning their offer of representation. Stay away from an "agent" who refuses to answer your questions, is rude or bullying, or pressures you in anyway.

- **Sending a generic acceptance form letter**
  When a legitimate agent offers to represent a client, she takes the time to make a personal telephone call or send a note to the author. A professional agent would never remit a representation offer using a generic form letter containing wording that could apply to any book – only con artists do that.

- **Unprofessional contract terms**
  Avoid agents with contracts that include perpetual agency clauses, claims on client's future commissions if the agency has no part in selling the property, billing clients for normal business expenses, provisions that ask for upfront payments, clauses for publishing through print-on-demand, or contracts that offer no advance.

- **Promises of publication**
  A literary agent, regardless of how well established he is, can never guarantee he will sell your book. Unsavory "agents" use promises of publication to entice trusting writers.

- **Lack of contacts**
  If an agent lacks publishing contacts, that is a red warning flag. Obviously, established agents have extensive networks of contacts, but even new agents are not new to publishing and have lists of contacts. Using the resources listed in Chapter 4, research an agent's background and experience. Consider asking the agent to list a few editors he thinks may be interested in your work and why he selected those particular contacts. If he cannot answer that question, find another agent.

Websites Predators & Editors (**anotherealm.com/prededitors**) and WriterBeware (**www.sfwa.org/for-authors/writer-beware**) each maintain a database of individual agents to avoid.

If you have been a victim of a scam or were misrepresented by an unscrupulous agent consider contacting the following resources for assistance:

- The Federal Trade Commission, Bureau of Consumer Protection investigates fraud. You may file a complaint on their Website at **www.ftc.gov**.

- Volunteer Lawyers for the Arts (**www.vlany.org**) offers guidance and answers to your legal questions.
- The Better Business Bureau's Website (**www.bbb.org**) allows you to search for information on a business as well as file a complaint.
- Contact your state's attorney general via **www.attorneygeneral.gov**.

The Author-Agent Agreement

Each agency has its own form of an author-agent agreement. You should understand and feel comfortable with the contract before you sign it. Ask the agent to clarify any terms or clauses you do not understand. You may also request reasonable changes. The author-agent agreement may outline, note, or include the following:

- Confirmation that your agent is the exclusive sales representative for your work.

- The right of your agent to hire co-agents to help sell subsidiary rights.

- The agent's responsibilities.

- What work your agent will represent (usually all of an author's literary works in all forms.)

- The duration of the agreement – some contracts have a specific period of time after which the author has the option to extend the contract or allow it to lapse.

- How notification must be submitted to terminate the contract. For instance, by certified letter with a thirty-day notice.

- The agent's right to represent competitive books.

- The amount of the agent's commission.

- Additional expenses you are responsible for (such as messenger service costs, the purchase of review galleys, or attorney's fees.)

- A clause stating that, upon request, you are entitled to receive an itemized list of expenses.

- The right of the agent to act as a conduit for payments received by the publisher.

- The remittance time for issuing payments to you after they are received from the publisher.

- You affirm that you have the right to allow the agent to sell the book. (In other words, you confirm that no one else can claim rights to the material.)

- A clause stating that, in the event of your death you have the right to assign the agreement to your heirs. This ensures that any outstanding royalties or income are paid to your estate.

- Which state's laws will be used to interpret the contract, should a dispute arise. Usually it is the state where the agent's office is located.

- The method that will be used to resolve disputes - for example, mediation, arbitration, or litigation.

- A clause stating that any changes to the agreement must be approved by both parties.

- Under what circumstances you can terminate the agreement – for example, this section may note what your responsibilities are if you leave before the contract expires.

- What your agent's rights and responsibilities are after the agreement ends – for instance, the agent may retain the right to sell subsidiary rights for any books she has sold while under contract.

How to protect yourself

If you are signing with a new agent who does not have an established reputation, you may wish to consider negotiating more specific terms designed to protect yourself should the agent be unable to sell your book or if you become unhappy with the relationship.

- **Include an exit clause**
  This clause allows you to terminate the contract should anything go wrong. If an agent agrees to this clause, he will most likely include a stipulation that should your book sell in the future to any of the publishers he pitched, the agent is entitled to the commission. The agent may also require an extended termination notice, such as 120 to 180 days.

- **Limit the term**
  If the agent does not agree to an exit clause, then insist upon a term limit which specifies a period of time (for instance, eighteen months) after which if the agent has not sold the book, the author has the option to seek alternate representation.

- **Add a key man clause**
  A key man clause specifies that should your agent leave the agency for another firm, you have the right to terminate the agreement.

- **Request a cap on expenses**
  If the agreement specifies that you are responsible for legitimate expenses incurred by the agency, ask for a cap to be placed on those expenses (for instance $300 or $500.)

- **Consider hiring an attorney**
  If you choose to hire an attorney to review the agreement it is important that the lawyer:

  1. Provide a fast turnaround time. You do not want to keep an agent waiting and risk having the offer rescinded (which is a common occurrence when lawyers become involved in the process.)

  2. Is an expert in book publishing and agent agreements. Do not obtain the services of a general 'entertainment' attorney, you need someone who is adept in the publishing industry.

  3. Outlines his points to you, so you can approach the agent to request the changes. Never have the attorney contact the agent directly.

  4. Cleary defines his fee prior to reviewing the material. You do not want to have any surprises later.

Chapter 10 | Getting the Book Deal

After you have hired a literary agent, the next step in your writing career is to try to land a book deal. Your book idea will go through many steps and stages before it is finally sold and published. You will also need to successfully navigate your relationship with your agent to keep it healthy and productive.

Selling the Book

Once the agency agreement is signed by both parties, the author-agent partnership is official and the process of selling your book to a publisher begins. The timeframe from when you first acquire an agent, through landing a book deal, to ultimately seeing your book in stores can vary dramatically and is based on numerous components. Following is a guideline of the steps involved with getting your book to market and a general timeline to help you understand the process.

Step 1: The agent will work with you to make edits to the proposal

Agents usually take on new projects they feel are strong enough to send out to publishers immediately. However, sometimes the agent will ask you to make edits and polish the proposal further before pitching it to publishing house editors.

Your agent may provide you an editorial letter outlining the requested changes, insert comments directly on your proposal, or - if the edits are minimal - simply discuss it with you in an informal telephone conversation. Depending on your agent's schedule, you may receive this within a few days or within several weeks. You and your agent will then determine a timeframe for when you will deliver the edits. Based on the scope of the changes, your material may go through several rounds of edits and may require a few days or weeks to complete.

Step 2: The agent will pitch the project to a list of carefully selected publishers

Once the material is strong enough to send out, the agent will write a pitch letter (similar to a query letter) and approach several publishers that she feels are good matches for your book. Most agents will pitch your project to more than one editor at the same time. Your agent may submit it to three editors or 40 editors simultaneously. Each individual agent has his or her own selling technique.

Do not expect your agent to share the list of the publishers she has approached, or is planning to pitch, until after the submission process is complete. An agent's job is to sell your book and most agents prefer not to consult with authors about who they should be pitching (unless a specific publisher has expressed an interest). It is best to let your agent do her job and not interfere with her pitching process. The timing of the submission stage varies greatly depending on how widely the work is submitted.

Step 3: When an offer is received, the agent will negotiate with the publisher on your behalf

It may take months or even years before you receive a publishing offer - or you may land a book deal the same day you hire your agent. There is no way to know how long it will take between the submission stage and the offer stage. Once a publisher does make a verbal offer, your agent will negotiate the major terms of the agreement with the editor. The negotiation process usually takes only a few hours to a few days to complete.

Step 4: The publisher will create a formal agreement

Once the terms have been negotiated, the publisher will construct a formal agreement. This may take two to twelve weeks.

Step 5: The agent may negotiate minor details of the agreement
Once the agent receives the formal publishing contract, she will review the details and may ask the publisher's legal department to make a few minor adjustments to the language contained in the agreement. This may add a few days to a few weeks to the timeline.

Step 6: The author and publisher sign the contract, after which an advance payment is issued
Once the final contract is agreed and signed by the author, the publisher will countersign it and issue your agent the initial portion (usually fifty-percent) of the negotiated advance payment. Your agent will take her commission from the payment, and send you the remaining balance. This stage of the process may take four to six weeks.

Step 7: The author completes and delivers the manuscript
The average publishing contract gives the author six to twelve months to deliver the final manuscript. Most nonfiction authors will begin writing the manuscript as soon as they receive a verbal offer from the publisher.

Step 8: Final edits are requested and delivered
Once you deliver the final manuscript, the editor will review the book and provide comments for final edits. The editor takes between two to ten weeks to provide the editing notes to you. Then you will make the final changes and resubmit it to the editor. Sometimes there will be several rounds of edits necessary.

Step 9: The book is put into production
Once the editor receives your final changes and the manuscript is 'approved', the publisher will send the second half of the advance payment to your agent, who will then issue you the payment, less her commission. Now your book goes into the production process, which consists of copyediting, proofreading, design, and printing.

The publication date of your book may be six to eighteen months after the manuscript is delivered and accepted (approved with final edits.)

Stages of the process	Timeframe
The agent requests edits to the proposal prior to submission to publishers.	One day to three weeks
The author makes the requested changes and returns the material to the agent.	One week to two months
The agent pitches the book to editors and receives an offer	A few hours to two years
The agent negotiates the terms of the verbal offer	One to seven days
The publisher issues a formal contract	Two to twelve weeks
The agent negotiates minor details of the agreement	One to four weeks
The author signs the contract and the initial portion of the advance payment is issued	Four to six weeks
The author delivers the completed manuscript to the publisher	Eight weeks to twelve months
The editor reviews the manuscript and requests edits	Two to ten weeks
The author makes changes and resubmits the manuscript	Two weeks to three months
The editor reviews the changes and approves the manuscript or requests additional edits	Two to six weeks (plus six to eight weeks if additional edits are requested)
The publisher issues the second half of the advance payment	Four to six weeks
The book goes into production and is published	Six to eighteen months

The Publishing Contract

Your agent will negotiate the terms for your publishing contract. Most agents deal with specific publishing houses so often that they already have a preset contract with the publisher that outlines agreed upon terms. Then all the agent needs to do is negotiate a few rights and terms particular to the author. The four most important areas the agent will negotiate on your behalf are:

1. The manuscript delivery and acceptance
2. The advance
3. Royalty payments
4. The subsidiary rights

Manuscript delivery and acceptance

The publishing contract will outline the date the manuscript must be delivered and stipulate that the publisher is only obligated to accept, pay for, and publish a manuscript that is satisfactory in form and content. Your agent will work with you to ensure the delivery date is practical and can be realistically met. She will also try to insert wording in the agreement that obligates the publisher to assist you in editing a specific number of drafts before the publisher can reject the manuscript.

The advance

An advance is the payment you receive prior to your book's publication. The advance is often based upon an estimate of your book's first year sales. The amount is an advance against future earnings. Advances range from $5,000 to $500,000. The advance is broken into two payments. One payment of fifty percent is issued at the time the contract is signed and the remaining payment is issued upon delivery and acceptance of the complete manuscript. Your agent will negotiate to get you the highest advance possible. Of course, the publisher wants to pay as small an advance as possible because they want to ensure the entire amount they pay you upfront will be earned back through your royalties. Since you do not have to return any of your advance - unless the book is cancelled due to the author breaching the contract - the publisher loses the portion of the advanced amount that you do not earn back through sales of your book.

Royalty payments

Your agent will ensure you earn royalties for sales of your book that are appropriate with industry standards. Most authors receive a royalty of 10 percent of the book's retail price for the first 5,000 copies sold, a royalty of 12 ½ percent of the book's retail price on the next 5,000 copies sold, and a royalty of 15 percent of the book's retail price on all copies sold after that. Your agent will make sure that the publisher provides a bi-annual accounting of your royalties.

Subsidiary rights

Subsidiary rights are all the rights (except for publishing rights) that are associated with your book that are available to sell. They include:

- **Reprint rights**
  Reprint rights grant the right to print the book in paperback edition. In most publishing agreements, the publisher retains the reprint rights.

- **Book club rights**
  There are numerous book clubs in existence that specialize in different genres and acquire book club rights to be able to offer your book to their members. Money made from the sales of book club rights is split equally between the author and the publisher.

- **Serial rights**
  A serial is an excerpt of your book that is reprinted in a

magazine or in another book, such as an anthology or compilation. First serial rights allow excerpts to be printed prior to the book's publication. Second serial rights grant the right to publish the excerpts after the book has been released. It is more common for nonfiction material to be serialized than fiction.

- **Foreign language rights**
  Your agent may use a co-agent in another country to capitalize on selling foreign language rights, which grant the right for your book to be printed in non-English speaking countries. Some publishing houses are already setup to publish in foreign countries. In this situation, your agent will allow the publisher to retain these rights knowing the foreign house will print your book.

- **Electronic rights**
  Electronic rights grant the right to publish the book electronically. An e-book published on the Internet or a book purchased to read on an electronic device is a form of electronic publishing.

- **Audio rights**
  Audio books often complement the printed version of the book. Audio rights refer to books that are published in audio form, such as on a cassette tape or compact disc, or delivered as an mp3, available for downloading from the Internet.

- **Performance rights**
  Performance rights allow your book to be made into a film, a television show, a video game, or a play or musical. An agent usually charges a 20 percent commission for the sales of performance rights.

- **Merchandising rights**
  Merchandising rights allow the creation of products related to your book, such as calendars, greeting cards, games, or toys.

How To Maintain a Successful Working Relationship with Your Agent

Agents hope to maintain positive, long-term relationships with the authors they represent. They are not looking to sell one writer's book and then move on to the next writer. An agent's goal is to create a successful partnership throughout a writer's career. Here are ways you can help sustain a healthy and prosperous relationship with your agent.

1. **Do not make unnecessary demands on your agent's time**
   Your agent has many clients and responsibilities to tend to throughout his day. Be considerate and do not consume his time with unnecessary interruptions by calling him every day, sending five e-mails an hour, or contacting him on the weekend to see if your book has sold, yet. Contact your agent when you have a legitimate reason to do so, not just to "check-in".

2. **Understand the agent's role**
   One your book is sold to a publisher and the contract has been successfully negotiated, the primary job of the agent is done. An agent can feel frustrated if an author does not understand the agent's role, which can create problems in the author-agent relationship. Do not expect your agent to also be your editor, your confidante, your sounding board, your coach, or your publicist.

   The role of your agent is to:
   - Sell your first book
   - Negotiate the terms of your publishing contract

- Explain business issues and contract details when you have questions
- Act as a middle-man should there be a dispute between you and your editor
- Campaign on your behalf if your editor leaves the publishing house
- Ensure you adhere to your publishing contract by delivering the manuscript on time and following the stipulations outlined under your option clause
- Sell subsidiary rights
- Strategize with you regarding the concept of your follow-up books and the overall vision for your career
- Sell your subsequent books

3. **Avoid micromanaging**
   Recognize that your agent is a professional with years of experience and knowledge – she doesn't need you telling her what to do. Respect your agent and let her do her job without interference.

4. **Never have someone else contact the agent on your behalf**
   You are the agent's client - not your assistant, not your attorney, not your writing coach, not your spouse, not your publicist, and not your accountant. The agent expects to deal directly with you and will quickly become annoyed if he is forced to connect with other people on your team.

5. **Do not take your agent for granted**
   Be appreciative of all the hard work your agent does on your behalf. Send a thank you note when she gives you advice, lands you a writing assignment, or sells your book. Remember, she represents you because she believes in you and your work. Be sure to acknowledge her efforts in your book's acknowledgements page.

6. **Share what you are doing to further your career**
   Keep your agent up-to-date. Send her a short note whenever something good happens – for instance, when you receive a prestigious award, land an appearance on The Today Show, or send off the final edits to the publisher.

7. **Be faithful to your agent**
   Your agent is committed to you, so be loyal to her.

8. **Retain a positive attitude**
   It may take a long time to sell your book. You need to trust your agent and have patience. Remain dedicated to your career and determined to succeed.

9. **Deliver what you promise, on time**
   If you are contracted to deliver an 80,000-word book, do not submit one that is only 35,000 words in length. If it is your responsibility to obtain special use permissions before your book is submitted, ensure you acquire all of them. If you stated you would supply fifteen images for use in the book, make sure you do so. If your publishing agreement stipulates that you deliver your completed manuscript within nine months, do not be late. Your contract is a legal document. You need to take it seriously because the publisher will. Do not agree to any terms that will be difficult for you to deliver. If you fail to deliver as promised, the publisher has the right to cancel your book. This reflects badly on the agent and hurts the relationship she has with the publisher and editor. The agent will not receive the remaining commission that she has earned and will be forced to return the commission she has already received. You will be forced to return the entire advance payment issued by the publisher, and will most likely no longer have an agent representing you.

10. **Work with your agent, not against him**

   Remember, your relationship with your agent is a partnership. You are both working toward the same goal – to sell you book and establish your writing career. When your agent makes suggestions, offers advice, or recommends accepting a specific deal, work with him, not against him. If you strongly disagree with his suggestions, advice, or recommendations, have a discussion with your agent regarding your opinion. Always keep the lines of communication open and respectful.

11. **Be wary of offering referrals**

   Do not offer your agent's name indiscriminately to other writers who are seeking representation. Your referrals reflect on you. Only offer a referral to an author you respect and feel would be a good fit with your agent.

When To Consider Ending The Author-Agent Partnership

If your book attains bestselling status, other agents will start contacting you. Prestigious agents from large firms may try to lure you away from your current agent. If your agent is doing a good job for you, think carefully before jumping ship for another agency. Remember, your agent believed in you and recognized your potential long before you achieved success – and she helped you become a published author.

However, there may be circumstances under which the partnership with your agent is no longer working and you may want to consider ending the relationship. Some of those legitimate reasons may be:

- **When there is poor communication**

   If your agent does not stay in regular contact with you or if she does not return your calls or e-mails, she may be overwhelmed with too many clients and unable to devote the time needed to further your career. You have a right to receive a response from your agent in a timely manner. If communication has broken down, it may be time to seek alternate representation.

- **When an agent lacks integrity**
  If she cannot explain her efforts to sell your work, if you catch her in a lie, if you suspect she participates in unethical practices, and you no longer trust your agent, it is time to move on.

- **When the agent is not productive**
  If you do not agree with her procedures, for instance if she does not share the responses she receives from publishers, if she only pitches to one editor at a time and waits four months for a response, or has her assistant discuss progress reports with you instead of doing it herself, then you must find an agent whose methodology is more conducive to your needs.

- **When the agent is not enthusiastic about your book**
  You need an agent who is fired up and passionate about your work. Someone who believes in your writing career and will diligently pitch your manuscript or book idea until it is sold. If your agent is not enthusiastic about your project, you need to find another agent who is.

Make a graceful exit
If you have done your best to attempt to resolve the issues with your agent – you have discussed it and tried to find a satisfactory remedy to the situation - and still the problems persist, you will need to formally end the business arrangement. It is best to exit the relationship with respect and professionalism. You do not want to become known as a difficult author who jumps from agent to agent. If your book has already been sold, your agent will

still be entitled to receive her earned commissions and represent the subsidiary rights, so you do not want to burn bridges. Move on with dignity and grace. Notify your agent of your decision by telephone (or in person, when possible) and then follow up with a certified letter confirming the new terms.

Becoming Successfully Published

The keys to becoming successfully published include continuing to develop your craft, learning everything you can about the publishing business, and never giving up. It may take years to acquire an agent or you may land a book deal tomorrow. Writers who stay focused and committed to their publishing goals are the ones who become published authors.

Jack Canfield and Mark Victor Hansen received 144 rejections for their book *Chicken Soup for the Soul*. Today it is the most successful and bestselling nonfiction series in publishing history.

Successful writers never give up. They diligently marketed themselves and their books until they become published authors - and you can too.

Agents and editors are desperate for quality authors and compelling books. They are under tremendous pressure to find promising new writers with books that will sell. There has never been a better time to be a writer. With the changing publishing world, agents and editors realize the importance of finding authors who understand the business, who are committed to a writing career, and who are able to connect directly with their potential readers. You can be one of the writers they are searching for.

Get Published! has shown you how to establish and build a platform, find and evaluate an agent that is right for you, create a winning query letter, and a convincing book proposal. This book has provided all the tools you need to navigate the publishing industry, hire an agent, and move forward on your path to becoming a published author.

Appendix I: National Writer's Conferences

Agents and Editors Conference
www.writersleague.org
Annual conference held each summer. Offers writers to the opportunity to meet with agents and editors.

ASJA Writers Conference
www.asjaconference.org
Annual conference held in April. Offers sessions on nonfiction writing.

Book Expo America
www.writersdigest.com/bea
Annual conference held in May. Offers instruction on the craft of writing and advice for submitting work.

La Jolla Writers Conference
www.lajollawritersconference.com
Annual conference held in October. Agents, editors, publishers, and publicists teach classes.

Maui Writers Conference
www.mauiwriters.com
Annual conference held Labor Day weekend. Sessions with agents and publishers, and one-on-one consultations available.

Writer's Digest Conference
www.writersdigestconference.com
Annual conference held in September. Sessions with agents, authors, and editors on the business of getting published.

Appendix II: Sample Book Proposal

(The actual proposal was double-spaced and included a sample chapter following the chapter outline and supplemental material.)

A Proposal for

MODERN TRADITIONS:
*Inspiring Ideas for Incorporating
Yesterday's Customs into Today's Wedding*

by Gina Cunningham

1234 Main Street
Anytown, USA
(310) 555-5555
gina@myemail.com

Table of Contents

Overview

Engaged couples want weddings that blend tradition and personal style. They are looking to the past for inspiring ways to transform a modern wedding into a meaningful experience.

Modern Traditions will be the first book to present traditional cultural wedding elements with a twist; updated and reinterpreted for today's couple. The book will outline cultural customs, rituals, and symbolism from around the world associated with music, dance, food, ceremony, design, and decor and provide inspiring ideas for readers to adapt traditions to their wedding.

Modern Traditions will help brides and grooms design a signature wedding that reflects their style as a couple by defining ways to honor their heritage, adopt a custom, update a tradition, or create a new ritual to personalize their wedding and pay elegant tribute to what is meaningful to them.

Industry publications and professionals note the trend toward incorporating, updating, and "borrowing" wedding traditions. *Bride's* magazine reports, "couples are choosing to observe centuries-old traditions, updating them to reflect their own personalities. And more couples than ever before are including ethnic customs from their heritages in wedding celebrations." *Modern Bride* magazine observes in their 2002 report, "couples are borrowing traditions from their own heritage or other cultures [for their wedding]."

Bridal Guide writes, "Many couples select traditions from a variety of cultures because the idea resonates with them. They like the symbolism behind these acts and incorporate them [into their wedding], regardless of the heritage." The book will provide a much-needed resource in the fast growing wedding design market. *Modern Traditions* will appeal to:

- Couples wanting to incorporate aspects of each other's culture into the wedding
- Couples looking for a guide to provide practical and stylish ideas for incorporating traditional elements into the wedding
- Couples looking for ideas to personalize their wedding
- Couples wanting to add meaningful elements to their wedding
- Couples wanting to differentiate their wedding from others and create a unique celebration
- Couples wanting to differentiate their wedding from others and create a unique celebration
- Wedding coordinators, designers, event planners, and catering managers looking for new ideas and inspiration

As a wedding coordinator and designer, the author has planned numerous celebrations incorporating her clients' cultures and personalities. From Irish hand-fastings to African-American ribbon tying, the author creates inspiring events for couples. The author will present ideas from her diverse portfolio and create new designs gathered from extensive cultural research.

Vibrant photographs of design elements, sidebars with real couples' stories, references to celebrities' wedding designs, checklists outlining updated ideas, and a complete resource list will add value and visual appeal.

The finished manuscript will contain 250 pages, including twenty pages of back matter, seventy-three photographs, and nineteen black and white photographs, and one chart. The book will be divided into three sections: ceremony, design, and celebration, with eighteen chapters, five design element inserts, and ten couples' stories. The manuscript will be completed six months after the book advance is received.

The author will ask the following authorities to write an introduction or cover quote:

- Colin Cowie, celebrity wedding designer, author, and television host
- Maria Melinger-McBride, wedding designer, author of *The Perfect Wedding* and *The Perfect*
- Vera Wang, celebrity wedding fashion designer and author
- Carley Roney, author *The Knot Guide to Wedding Traditions and Vows*, creator TheKnot.com

Back matter will include a resource list, a chart of traditions by culture, recommended reading, author's biography, and a form for the readers to note their design ideas, photo credits, a feedback request form, and index

Spin-offs
Modern Traditions will be the first in a series of six wedding design books including:
- A Heritage Wedding: Culturally Inspired Designs to Personalize Your Wedding
- Elegant Themes: Stylish Designs to Personalize Your Wedding
- Defining Your Wedding Style: How To Reveal Your Personality to Design a Unique Celebration
- Inspired Ideas for Designing an Elegant Wedding on a Minimal Budget
- Stylish Ideas for Designing a Destination Wedding

Market

More than 2.4 million couples marry each year in the United States according to *Modern Bride*. The Great Bridal Expo reports that weddings are a $92 billion per year industry. Gerard Monaghan, president of the Association of Bridal Consultants, adds that wedding inquiries are up 25% since September 11, 2001 and states, "[according to a survey of 2,600 professional wedding coordinators] there is a growing demand for weddings celebrating heritage."

According to the Great Bridal Expo, wedding customers are 90% female, age 25-34, college graduates, with an average combined income level of $75,000. Engaged consumers are recession proof, constantly renewing, and have high immediate needs. Couples purchase wedding items at bridal fairs, wedding salons, event showrooms, and stationary stores, and via the internet. A bride spends over 100 hours designing the wedding. Brides turn to design books, wedding experts, bridal magazines, and television shows for inspiration.

Markets for the book include engaged couples and members of the hospitality industry: wedding designers, coordinators, and venue catering managers.

Promotion

   The author will do the following to help the publisher promote the book:

Publicity Campaign
Expand the author's current publicity campaign by hiring a public relations firm with expertise in book promotion to obtain national television interviews and magazine and newspaper features.

Media Kit & Video
Expand the author's current media kit. Press kit will include the author's biography, headshot, book cover jacket (galley), author Q&A sheet, Rolodex card, book reviews, and press clippings. Author will hire award-winning videography company Blvd. Video Productions to produce an 8-minute video featuring author interviews and wedding design highlights. Produce 1,000 Rolodex cards with "wedding expert" headline to be sent to media and journalists. Author will commission Century Guild Press to create a letterpress media box to hold the press kit, video, and tie-in promotional items. Author will make press kit and her media contact list available to the publisher.

Send Books to Opinion-Makers
If publisher supplies copies of the books, the author will mail twenty-five books to leading wedding industry opinion-makers.

Author Magazine Articles and Column
Pitch author-written feature articles to media contacts at national wedding magazines including *Martha Stewart Weddings, Bridal Guide, Modern Bride, Conde' Nast Bride's*, and *Elegant Bride*. Pitch a "Modern Traditions" column to *Elegant Bride Magazine*.

Television Special

Approach production company contacts to produce a television special based on *Modern Traditions*. With the author's association with Lifetime Television, the network would be a good placement for the show.

Obtain Appearances on Design Shows and Wedding Shows

Contact design and wedding shows to be a featured expert. Shows include: Martha Stewart Living (CBS), You're Invited (Style Network), Weddings of a Lifetime (Lifetime Television), InStyle Wedding Special (NBC), and other current wedding shows in production.

Bridal Fairs

Author will provide 20,000 book postcards (with book cover and purchase information) to The Great Bridal Expo. The postcards will be used as "bag stuffers" and handed to attendees at eighteen national bridal fairs located in: Philadelphia, New York City, Washington D.C., Baltimore, Long Island, Boston, Detroit, Dallas, Miami, Atlanta, Fort Lauderdale, San Francisco, Anaheim, Los Angeles, Denver, Phoenix, Cleveland, and Cincinnati. Author will give The Great Bridal Expo thirty-six copies (two copies per city) of Modern Traditions to be given as prizes to attendees. Author will conduct "Modern Traditions" workshops at select bridal shows.

Wedding and Event Industry Conferences

Author will attend, speak, and sell books at the four leading wedding and event industry conferences each year: The Special Event (sponsored by the International Special Events Society), The Business of Brides (sponsored by the Association of Bridal Consultants), Event Solutions, and the National Association of Catering Executives.

Website

Expand the author's current website to include an updated author appearance schedule for television and magazine features, creative wedding ideas and tips, links to bookseller's website to purchase the book, author's biography, press page (for media to contact the author), resources for purchasing wedding items associated with the book, and a monthly contest to win a one-hour telephone consultation with the author. Promote the book online with "live chats" or interviews with AOL's writer's club, amazon.com writer interviews, barnesandnoble.com, theknot.com, weddingchannel.com, modernbride.com, and Martha Stewart Weddings online.

About the Author

As a celebrated wedding designer, coordinator, and owner of Wedding Design Studio in Los Angeles, Ms. Cunningham creates and produces distinctive weddings for couples. Her diverse portfolio includes both celebrity couples (actors and prominent sports figures) and everyday couples.

She has been featured on several episodes of Lifetime Television's "Weddings of a Lifetime," The Today Show, and Good Morning, America. Ms. Cunningham writes a bi-monthly column on theme weddings for *Inside Weddings Magazine* and speaks to more than 50,000 event professionals at conferences each year.

Her blog, Designing Poetic Weddings, receives more than 5,000 hits per day and she has a database of 85,000 subscribers for her monthly e-newsletter. Ms. Cunningham has been featured in *Elegant Bride Magazine, Bridal Guide, Conde Nast Bride's WeddingBells, The Knot WeddingPages, InStyle Magazine, Martha Stewart Weddings*, and *The Los Angeles Times*.

Comparable Competitive Analysis

There are no competitive books currently on the market that explore cultural customs and provide updated interpretations and ideas for incorporating them into the wedding design. The books that would most closely compete with *Modern Traditions* are:

The Knot Guide to Wedding Vows and Traditions: Readings, Rituals, Music, Dance, Speeches, and Toasts by Carley Roney, Broadway Books, 2000, paperback, 200 pages, $15.00. A bestseller in Theknot.com series. Provides cultural and religious wedding suggestions. Book does not provide design ideas or update traditions. Topics are limited to wedding readings, toasts, speeches, ceremony vows, and music selection.

A Bride's Book of Wedding Traditions: A Treasury of Ideas for Making Your Wedding The Most Memorable Day Ever by Arlene Hamilton Stewart, Hearst Books, 1995, 4 printings, hardcover, 300 pages, $18.00. Details the history of marriage and the origins of wedding custom. Only covers English and American traditions. Provides only a few design ideas. No photos.

Timeless Traditions: A Couple's Guide to Wedding Customs Around the World by Lisl M. Spangenberg, Universe, 2001, paperback, 232 pages, $22.50. An extensive, though not exhaustive, collection of cultural wedding traditions, sorted by country. Customs and traditions are outdated and impractical. Author does not provide design ideas or suggestions for updating customs for the modern bride. No photos.

Chapter Outline

Acknowledgements
Introduction
Chapter 1:   Getting Accustomed

SECTION ONE: CEREMONY
Chapter 2:   Custom Tailored –
                Wedding Attire, Rings, and Accessories
Chapter 3:   When December Snows Fall Fast –
                Wedding Location, Date and Time
Insert 1:   The Ties That Bind – *Wedding Knots*
Chapter 4:   Embracing the Sun –
                Rites of Passage and Pre-Wedding Celebrations
Chapter 5:   Quill and Ink – *Invitations and Programs*
Insert 2:   To Speak of Love – *Poetry, Quotes, and Readings*
Chapter 6:   Angels on Horseback – *Wedding Transportation*
Chapter 7:   Ceremonia – *The Ceremony Elements*

SECTION TWO: DÉCOR AND DESIGN
Chapter 8:   Walking Among The Stones – *Ceremony Décor*
Chapter 9:   Lavender and Edelweiss –
                Bouquets and Boutonnieres
Chapter 10:   Of Branches and Ivy – *Wreaths and Garlands*
Insert 3:   Illumination – *Candles and Fire*
Chapter 11:   Cattails and Harvest Wheat – *Setting the Table*
Chapter 12:   Of Heaven and Earth – *Design Details*
Insert 4:   A Sweet Life – *Honey*
Chapter 13:   Red Boxes and Wishing Stones –
                Gifts, Favors, and Keepsakes

Chapter 1
Getting Accustomed

The first chapter discusses why couples include traditions in their weddings, then goes on to give readers an understanding of how to incorporate traditions into the wedding. It outlines universal elements and provides options for honoring one's culture, updating traditions, blending cultures and traditions, borrowing traditions, and creating new traditions. The chapter explains the importance of intent in creating new rituals and gives "how-to's" for getting started, finding inspiration, selecting items, and designing the flow of elements to run smoothly. The author provides specific ideas for sharing the significance of the traditions with the wedding guests. The chapter concludes by encouraging readers to explore and identify what is important to them as a couple.

SECTION ONE – CEREMONY

Chapter 2
Custom Tailored: Wedding Attire, Rings, and Accessories
   Chapter two outlines traditional wedding attire, accessories, and rings by culture and provides stylish ideas for incorporating and updating elements. The chapter begins with wedding clothes: dresses (colors, style, embroidery, symbolism, fabrics, patterns), heirloom gowns, groom's attire, wedding attendant's clothes, and shoes; and then discusses hairstyles, special tokens, veils and headpieces, accessories, handkerchiefs, and ribbons. A section on rings: types of rings (including Claddagh, Gimmal, posie, Celtic, Luckenboot, crested, gemstones, precious stones, birthstones, keeper rings, regard rings, and Fede rings), engraving rings, and meanings associated with rings completes the chapter. "A Couple's Story" features Melissa and David: A Wedding with English, Asian, African-American, Israeli, and Celtic elements.

Chapter 3
When December Snow Falls Fast: Wedding Location, Date, and Time
   In Victorian times, falling snow on a couple's wedding day was believed to signify a happy marriage. "When December's snow falls fast
   The chapter outlines traditional wedding sites and selection of the wedding date and time. Traditions are listed by culture; ideas are provided for incorporating and updating them. Items included in the chapter are: outdoor weddings, historical venues, sacred places, divination techniques using fortune-tellers and astrologers, benefits of seasonal wedding celebrations, and preferred days and time. "A Couple's Story" features Jennifer and Lee: A Wedding with Filipino and Irish Elements and a beach theme.

Special Insert 1
The Ties That Bind: Wedding Knots
   Knots are one of the oldest and universal wedding elements. The special insert elaborates on numerous ways to creatively incorporate knots into the wedding. Highlights include: harvest knots, ribbon knots, bouquet knots, cookie knots, wrist knots, and handfasting knots.

Chapter 4
Embracing the Sun: Rites of Passage and Pre-Wedding Celebrations
   On the morning of her wedding a Native-American bride greets the sun in a ritual representing her passage into a new life.
   The chapter explores the universal practice of purification and transformation rituals, and provides ways to incorporate and update elements for the modern bride and groom. Highlights include henna and body painting, beauty applications, cleansing and symbolic baths, fragrant massages, wedding eve dinners, wedding showers, bachelor and bachelorette parties, engagement parties, and spiritual preparation ceremonies. "A Couple's Story" features Moira and Andrew: A Wedding with Native-American and French elements.

Chapter 5:
Quill and Ink: Invitations and Programs
   With quill and ink, medieval monks inscribed the first paper invitations in calligraphy.
   The chapter showcases invitation customs by culture, ways to elegantly update them, and the inclusion of cultural traditions. The chapter proposes ancient design options: engraving, calligraphy, letterpress, oral biddings, heraldry, coats of arms, emblems, and artwork and moves on to items included in an invitation and program: myths, legends, family stories, photos and

renderings, gifts and tokens, and the symbolism and significance of selected elements. The chapter closes by emphasizing the visual importance the invitation and program have on the wedding.

Insert 2:
To Speak of Love: Poetry, Quotes, and Readings
   The special insert focuses on how to use poetry, quotes and readings throughout the wedding design: invitations, programs, place cards, favors, toasts, and the ceremony.

Chapter 6:
Angeles on Horseback: Wedding Transportation
   A Corsican bride rides a white horse to her wedding ceremony. Along the way, she launches an olive branch down a stream to signify the abundance, peace, and happiness that will flow through her marriage.
   The chapter will list traditional, unique ways couples, and their guests, are transported to the wedding: horses, carriages, sleighs, foot, and specialty vehicles.

Chapter 7:
Ceremonia: The Ceremony Elements
   The chapter identifies cultural ceremony elements and suggests ways to update, borrow, and personalize them to create a meaningful and memorable event. The chapter begins with the bridal path, processional, and fire rituals, then details ceremony exchanges, sharing rituals, bindings and hand-fastings, offerings, and acceptance practices. The chapter concludes with unification ceremonies, rituals for honoring the family, symbolic tosses, and the recessional. "A Couple's Story" features Rebekah and Brooks: A Wedding with Celtic and Medieval elements.

SECTION TWO: DÉCOR AND DESIGN

Chapter 8:
Walking Among The Stones: Ceremony Décor
Stones have long been associated with wedding ceremonies and incorporated into the décor. To show her acceptance of the groom and commitment to the marriage, an Apache bride walks along a path of stones.

The chapter outlines traditional ceremony décor by culture and offers ways to create new designs. Starting with the creation of the altar, the chapter then moves on to canopies, banners, circles, stones, and the aisle. Recommendations for ceremony gifts and guest participation are included.

Chapter 9:
Lavender and Edelweiss: Bouquets and Boutonnieres
Boutonnieres are a legacy from medieval times when a knight would wear a flower or other item to match his lady's' colors.

The traditional use and origin of bouquets and boutonnieres is discussed. A thorough list of flowers and herbs is presented by culture, country of origin, season, color, and associated meanings and symbolism. "A Couple's Story" features Monica and Bernd: A Wedding with German, Southern, and African-American elements.

Chapter 10:
Of Branches and Ivy: Wreaths and Garlands
Wedding wreaths symbolize the circle of life. Ivy, representing fidelity, happiness, and marriage, and branches considered life's essence, are commonly incorporated into the floral design.

Chapter ten builds on chapter nine; elaborating on flowers and herbs used in wreaths and garlands. Hair wreaths, door wreaths, plant talismans, and necklace garlands are discussed.

Insert 3:
Illumination: Candles and Fire
   The special insert looks at the traditional, universal use of fire in wedding rituals and offers suggestions for bringing it into today's celebrations. Candlelit ceremonies, favors, and centerpieces are presented along with new traditions and ideas.

Chapter 11:
Cattails and Harvest Wheat: Setting the Table
   Traditionally, wedding celebrations were often held during autumn, after the harvest. Cattails and sheaves of wheat, seasonal items and fertility symbols, were frequent décor elements.
   The décor of the table is the focus of chapter eleven. First, table styles, sizes, and room placement are examined, followed by a presentation of fabric treatments, linens, and napkins. Next, we look at centerpieces, dishware, and glasses. An investigation of table display items completes the chapter. "A Couple's Story" features Yu Mei and Jeffrey: A Wedding with Chinese and Latin elements,

Chapter 12:
Of Heaven and Earth: Design Details
   Asian weddings abound with myth, symbolism, and balance: yin and yang, mirth and harmony, and heaven and earth – represented in the wedding décor by white paper tablets.
   The chapter elaborates on the design details: furnishings, lighting, and artistic elements. Colors, their meanings and significance, are examined by culture. Cultural symbols – butterflies, feathers, and maypoles – are explored for inspiration and creativity. Designing place cards, using ribbons, and displaying hope chests round out the chapter.

Insert 4:
A Sweet Life: Honey
   Another common wedding element, honey, is investigated in the special insert. Suggestions for bringing honey into your wedding in a playful and poignant way are provided. Ceremony tastings, décor, favors, and menu items are included.

Chapter 13:
Red Boxes and Wishing Stones: Gifts, Favors, and Keepsakes
   In an old Celtic tradition, guests throw pebbles into a river near the ceremony site, while making a wish for the couple. An updated version of this time-honored ritual will create a beautiful keepsake for the bride and groom: at the ceremony location, have guests place small stones, along with their wishes, in a glass container filled with water that you can keep in your new home.
   The chapter identifies traditional gifts and favors for guests, by country, provides inspiring suggestions for including unique items, and expands on ways to create meaningful keepsakes. Guest writings, family ties, and charitable contributions are covered, along with dozens of distinctive ideas. "A Couple's Story features Sumi and Matt: A Wedding with Indian and European elements.

SECTION THREE: CELEBRATION

Chapter 14:
Fiddlers, Pipers, and Ragamuffins: Music, Dance, and Entertainment
   In a rural Irish custom, it is considered a sign of good luck if strawboys or ragamuffins "attend" the cerebration and dance with the bride.
   The chapter explores music, dance, and entertainment associated with each culture. Instrumentation, guest participation, and the hiring of entertainers are discussed. A

comprehensive list of music and dances is included. "A Couple's Story" features Adrienne and Bud: A Wedding with Scottish and Hawaiian elements.

Chapter 15:
Wild Berries and Whiskey: Food and Wine
   Honor your heritage, include a favorite beverage, or create a unique twist on an age-old cultural item by providing whiskey shots (a traditional celebratory drink of Ireland and Scotland) during the cocktail hour or as a champagne substitute in the ritual wedding toast.
   The chapter outlines traditional drinks, wedding food, and dining customs by culture. The chapter begins with selecting the right type of meal service for your wedding: brunch, tea, breakfast, cocktails, dinner, or buffet and then expands on the ideas for the cocktail hour, lists sample menus, and suggestion on how to include family recipes. The chapter closes by exploring different cuisines for inspiration. "A Couple's Story" features Jane and Sachin: A Wedding with Indian and Irish elements.

Chapter 16:
To Taste Abundance: The Wedding Cake
   The wedding cake or bread is used worldwide to encourage fertility, wish the couple a sweet life, and offer a taste of the abundance a marriage will produce.
   The chapter focuses on traditional cakes by culture, helping the couple design one that represents their style and personality. The use of charms, trinkets, and ribbons is discussed along with selecting a filling and including a cake topper. The chapter concludes with the groom's cake.

Insert 5:
Rosemary for Remembrance: Herbs
 The final special insert focuses on the age-old tradition of wedding herbs. Herbal significance and symbolism along with dozens of suggestions for incorporating herbs into the wedding are highlighted. Design suggestions include herbal rings for votives, wine glasses and candles, herbal ribbons and ties, centerpieces, bouquets, boutonnieres, favors, and tosses.

Chapter 17:
Dancing on the Embers: Reception Customs
 At Belgium wedding celebrations, the bride and groom symbolically toss their past life onto the embers of a dying fire.
 The chapter identifies reception traditions from around the world. Highlights include toasts, the sharing of food and drink, and customs that honor family and ancestors. "A Couple's Story" features Narelle and Jacopo: A Wedding with Australian, Italian, and Jamaican elements.

Chapter 18:
Bringing the Wedding Vision to Life
 The final chapter offers guidance for pulling all the elements together and provides organizational steps, resources, and design forms to complete the process.

Glossary of Terms

Advance: payments made to a writer by the publisher prior to the book's publication. An advance is calculated against the estimated future sales of the book and is usually paid in installments.

Book Proposal: a detailed presentation of a nonfiction book's concept and marketing potential. It is used to acquire an agent and sell a book idea to a publisher.

Book Reviewer: a person who provides critiques and evaluations of literary works.

Copyediting: the act of reviewing a manuscript to ensure accuracy in writing style, grammar, punctuation and arrangement.

Copyright: the legal right of ownership of a written work.

Editor: a person who works at a publishing house, acquires projects, and coordinates the process of publication.

Endorsement or **Testimonial:** a written statement praising the content of the book.

Exclusive: offering a manuscript or book proposal to only one agent for a set-period and guaranteeing no one else may consider it during the exclusivity period.

Film Rights: rights sold or optioned by an agent to allow a book to be made into a film.

Foreign Rights: rights that allow the book to be reprinted or translated outside the United States.

Foreword: a section of a book written by an expert in the field or a celebrity to introduce the topic.

Galleys: copies of the book's interior layout for proofing prior to print.

Imprint: the name used to identify a publisher's specific line of books. Imprints are a separate line of products within a publishing house.

Interior layout: the design of the inside of the book, including placement of chapter titles, images, and other material.

ISBN (International Standard Book Number): A 10-digit number that is linked to and identifies the title and publisher of a book. It appears on the back of all books, as well as the dust jacket and the copyright page.

Library of Congress Catalog Number: a number used by the Library of Congress to identify books it includes in its collection. The number is used by libraries to order and catalog books.

Literary Agent: a person who acts on behalf of an author to sell his or her book to a publisher, negotiate contracts, and deal with subsidiary rights. Though agents are not lawyers, their experience working with publishing agreements provides the necessary knowledge to negotiate contracts for their clients.

Multiple Submissions: submitting several pitches for different projects to one agent at the same time. Agents will reject an author who sends multiple submissions.

One-Time Rights: rights that allow a portion of a book to be published again (for instance, in a magazine) without violating the contract.

Option Clause: a clause in a contract granting the publisher the right to release an author's subsequent books.

Platform: a writer's media exposure (through blogs, speaking engagements, interviews) and abilities to develop a potential group of readers.

Publisher: the company that releases / publishes a book.

Query Letter: a letter submitted to an agent to pitch the author and garner interest in a book project.

Reprint Rights: the right to republish a book after its initial print run.

Royalties: a percentage of the retail price that is paid to the author for each copy of the book that is sold.

Serial Rights: the rights granted to a magazine or paper to publish a portion of a book.

Simultaneous Submission: submitting the same query letter or book proposal to several agents at the same time.

Solicited: a book proposal that has been requested by the agent.

Subsidiary Rights: All rights, except for book publishing rights, listed in a publishing contract. These may include book club rights, paperback rights, and film rights.

Unsolicited: a book proposal sent to an agent without prior permission.

UPC (Universal Product Code) Bar Code: a 12-number code imprinted on retail products (including books) to track trade items.

About The Author

Laura Cross is an author, and a former professional ghostwriter and author strategist, who helped clients establish their expertise by becoming published authors and leveraging their knowledge for more profits, more prospects, and major media. Her author-clients appeared on *Oprah, The Today Show*, and *CNN*, were featured in *People* magazine, *Entrepreneur, Publishers Weekly*, and *The New York Times* book review section, and landed on Amazon's bestseller list. Laura currently runs Rebel Seed Films & Entertainment, an independent film company and boutique publishing firm.

Printed in Great Britain
by Amazon